TRENDS
BEYOND LIFE
In Search Of Immortality

by Susan Muncey

Wykham Books

A Wykham Book
ISBN 0-9511745-1-7
978-0-9511745-1-7

This edition published 2006-10-28
Copyright © Susan Muncey

Set in Perpetua 12/18

Published by Wykham Books, Chateau le Theron, 46170 Cézac, France
Printed and bound in Great Britain by Biddles Ltd, Kings Lynn, Norfolk

Papers used in the manufacture of this book are natural, recyclable products
made from wood grown in sustainable softwood forests.

CONTENTS

INTRODUCTION

PART ONE: LIFE TRENDS

18   Predicting the Future – *The Reality*

29   The Disposable Lifestyle of a Virtual World – *Dealing with Rapid Cultural Change*

ESSENTIALS FOR REAL LIFE - THE BACKLASH

45   Rights vs Responsibilities – *Coping with a 'New Morality'*

56   The Competitive Edge – *Winning in a Changing Global Marketplace*

61   Wars of the Future? - *Re-assessing Relationships in a Time of Dramatic Social Change*

71   Baby Blues – *The Future of Marriage and Family Life*

79   Gambling our Future Away – *"Destructional" Change and the Debt we Owe*

92   The Quest for Eternal Youth and Beauty – *Breaking Biological Barriers to Change*

103   The Future of Death – *Changing the History of Mortality*

PART TWO: DEATH TRENDS

114   Handling the Dead – *The Historical Legacy in Britain*

120   A Fresh Approach to Death – *The Ecological Perspective*

137   Bereavement and Immortality – *Experiences from the UK*

162   Experiences from the Developing World – *Death in Zambia*

MORTALITY AND AIDS

FUNERALS

BEREAVEMENT AND IMMORTALITY

199   Transcendence – *Expressions of Eternal Love*

208   A Look Beyond Physical Matter – *The Key to Everlasting Life?*

BIBLIOGRAPHY

We shall not cease from exploration
And the end of all our exploring
Will be to arrive where we started
And know the place for the first time

TS Eliot, 4 Quartets

INTRODUCTION

What started out as a personal interest in trends affecting our lives has now turned into several businesses. I call myself a futurologist, which probably means I'm just plain eccentric and I even coined the word "*visuology*" to describe my own unique approach to looking at the future. Visuology is in fact a combination of inspiration and guidance – a way of using predictions to help harness change when everything around us is in a state of flux. Over the years I've pored over books and hoarded countless newspaper and magazine cuttings about things that matter to me. With several decades of information stored up in my mental CPU (head), plus the inestimable help of the Internet, together with some hands-on research, I've finally recorded some of my observations - and added in some analysis and predictions for good measure.

The first thing I will mention is that predicting the future ain't so easy! When we wonder how our world might be in years to come we're often influenced by the stuff of fantasy. I'm not personally a great fan of the sci-fi genre but a lot of it is also based upon predicting future states of our existence. These days science fiction has become something of an academic discipline, distinguishing between ideas that are theoretically possible and those that are already known: such as travelling faster than the speed of light or replicating the way the sun creates energy through nuclear fusion. If it's evident that such ideas aren't possible they simply become out of date and - let's face it - nothing dates like the future.

Science fiction is somewhat like futurology – except that in my discipline we deal with the facts of reality rather than the wild imaginings of fantasists (sorry guys!). In focusing on the possible, science fiction often reflects our wants (yes, it would be very convenient to have flying cars and extremely useful to have robots to do all our work) and our fears (how many doomsday scenario films have you endured from the edge of your seat?) But science fiction didn't predict either mobile phones or the Internet, both of which have become vital to people across the globe. Science fiction is couched in the language of technology and appears to represent a scientific standpoint but it also relies upon the imagination of the author however vivid that may be. Most important of all - it's not true!

Futurology on the other hand is about analysing the multi-faceted aspects of our lives and making conclusions about the future that, although to some degree based on gut instinct, also derive from solid research. It is not limited to questions about our scientific future but spans all human experience including history, geography, economics and biology as well as our artistic, social and emotional transformation over time.

But enough of the background: you can read more of the history of futurology and its uses in Chapter One. I've chosen to divide this book into two sections - life trends and death trends - although these are inextricably linked to each other by one major force: the power of digital communication. Some say that the Internet is the most powerful invention since the wheel. It certainly affects every area of our lives: from our education to our day-to-day business, from our personal relationships to our international relations, from the way we source information to the way we conduct trade, from the way we present ourselves to the world whilst we are alive, to the way we are remembered after we are gone.

The increasingly fast pace of life in the developed world and the overwhelming variety of information and of choices available to us means that we are living at a time when the amount of change affecting our lives is often terrifying. The rapid and recent breakdown of tradition and convention in social communities in the Western world together with the emergence of a culture of disposability have led to traumatic changes in morality, creating widespread social disruption and emotional confusion.

Currently in the so-called developed world there is a trend towards expressing individuality. Such a thing was usually denied to us in the past when we had to conform to the rules of society, fight wars or find ways of feeding ourselves. In April 1998, Norman Tebbit wrote in the *Mail on Sunday* "*We have a new generation of adults who have never grown up. They have not been disciplined and do not know self-discipline. Having not been brought up to accept responsibility, they are irresponsible... they blur reality with unreality with drugs, or virtual reality...they confuse desire with affection, father children, but duck out of the responsibilities of fatherhood.*" Sogyal Rinpoche refers to something that he calls '*active laziness*' which we can probably all identify with: "*The Eastern style consists of hanging out all day in the sun, doing nothing, avoiding any kind of work or useful activity, drinking cups of tea, listening to music blaring on the radio, and gossiping with friends.*" Western laziness is different "*It consists of cramming our lives with compulsive activity so that there is no time to confront real issues.*"

The order of our relationships has also been disrupted by new freedoms and a more tolerant, liberal society. On the one hand huge numbers of barely educated single parent mothers depend on state benefits while highly intelligent women put off having children until it's too late because they're 'still trying to find out how they really feel.' The institution of marriage is also breaking down under the stresses of modern life and the realisation that men are no longer necessary for financial security or parenting. Women are becoming less forgiving and men can no longer expect the unconditional devotion that stems from inbuilt female resilience to cope with childbirth and raise offspring. Women have been socially programmed to tolerate and try to help men who may wish to use them as domestic staff, who are sometimes lazy and careless of their appearance, who possibly drink too much, snore like pigs and who are occasionally and - if found out - apologetically, unfaithful to them. The power of the newly independent *überwoman* is reflected in her tenacity; for instance her passionate desire to fight her corner in divorce cases and increasingly win vast sums of money, usually earned by her 'unsatisfactory' male partner.

Although two thirds of the world still exists without electricity and the majority of the global population lives in comparative poverty, the balance of our whole world order is also changing rapidly with China and India emerging as major economic players. Meanwhile, just as Internet casinos have suddenly become huge business we are simultaneously gambling our planet away through excessive and unregulated use of a diminishing supply of fossil fuels. Yet, ironically, it seems that we expect to live forever! The quest for eternal youth has us queuing up for cosmetic surgery, injections of growth hormones – and now there's even talk of *"brain lifts"* to pep up the ageing cranium – a new lifestyle choice for those with sufficient funds?

Despite huge increases in relative wealth and life-expectancy, it seems that we aren't any happier. Researchers recently found that when it comes to happiness Britain is ranked below twenty other nations – including some that are much poorer such as Uruguay, Ghana and Colombia. Studies show that, once basic needs (such as food in the fridge, clothes on your back, or a roof over your head) are met, surplus income does not increase happiness. Perhaps this is what lies behind leader of the UK Conservative Party David Cameron's utilitarian proposals to focus on the GWB (general well being) of the country's population, rather than its GDP, and the recent efforts of schools to teach pupils 'cheeriness and contentment'. The sad truth is that a modern lifestyle can be a lonely existence.

Some are seeking solace in their pets – in 2005, the American public spent $34 million on their dogs, cats, birds, fish and other creatures according to the American Pet Products Manufacturers Association. Pets are also becoming brand extensions of their owners – the way Paris Hilton dresses her Chihuahua is apparently *'an expression of herself'*. In fact, nowadays, you don't even need a real pet – just go to www.neopets.com, where more than 70 million people have already created their own cyber-companions thus avoiding those irritating responsibilities like feeding, walking and grooming. As Edward Castronova points out *"In online games, it is more possible, now, for every person to have at least a few moments of feeling truly accomplished, befriended and loved."*

The value of genuinely caring relationships, of true friendship, of a sense of purpose in life seem somehow to have been lost as we scrabble to earn enough to look like a celebrity to buy the latest gadgets or luxury designer branded goods. Take the case of Joyce Vincent, the 40 year old, who worked for the advertising agency, Saatchi & Saatchi. In January 2006, her skeleton was found in her north London bedsit where she had died more than two years ago. The skeleton was clutching a shopping bag and surrounded by Christmas presents she had wrapped but failed to deliver. The television and heating were still on. The housing officers who found her had come to repossess her flat because the rent was thousands of pounds in arrears. There were no suspicious circumstances surrounding the death. But where were her family, friends, workmates, or neighbours?

The second half of this book focuses on death trends – maybe better called immortality trends. In the West, death has become a taboo subject, due largely to vastly increased life expectancy that makes death seem a relatively alien phenomenon further compounded by centuries of social training or emotional repression. My friends and relatives thought I was going insane when I started investigating everything to do with death and funerals. Their quizzical looks appeared to conceal a suspicion that I had developed some macabre or voyeuristic obsession. Yet I was just discovering that we are running out of space in cemeteries - not just in parts of the world where AIDS and other diseases are endemic, but also here in London. Harriet Harman, the minister currently responsible for cemeteries says she is willing to tackle a massive political taboo by approving double-decker burials. Under her authority, untended graves more than 75 years old would be reopened, the remains would be removed and transferred to a smaller container, then reburied deeper in the same plot. New coffins would then be lowered into the same space. With 600,000 people dying every year Britain's cemeteries are full. The London boroughs of Hackney and Tower Hamlets for example have already run out of land and many families have to travel to find plots. Meantime, it's hardly surprising that the burial business is booming as became evident from my interview with Donald Boddy, award-winning designer and owner of an innovatively planned and beautifully landscaped remembrance park in the

Wirral in Cheshire. Needless to say pet cemeteries are also becoming big business.

I was also keen to find out about people's experience of bereavement and to contrast the experiences of those in the West with those in the developing world where death is much more a part of daily life – as documented following a research trip to Zambia. The ceremony and formality of the religious treatment of death varies from culture to culture, according to faith and its level of observance but rather than analyse these differences, I have observed how our general approach to death is changing, largely due to globalisation and especially due to the Internet.

Moreover it is sadly the case that many of us believe that immortality is attainable through wealth and fame. This is perhaps evidence of what the American writer Christopher Lasch calls '*the culture of narcissism.*' Lasch defines this as a waning of a sense of historical time, a flight from objective reality and seriousness, an addiction to success rather than achievement, a yearning for escapist solutions, overweening vanity and an imperative for immediate self-fulfilment rather than self-denial. This is apparent in young people's impatience to become successful in their careers, to achieve wealth and fame with neither hard work nor talent - and is based on a delusional sense of entitlement. In the youth-focused world of today most kids seem to think they have the right to anything they want which of course means that they'll all become footballers, models, pop or movie stars. A great deal of bitterness and disappointment is likely to result especially if the footballers, models, pop and movie stars of today are not the most perfect role models themselves.

In this age where many have become celebrity and brand obsessed it is almost as if immortality has become the ultimate purchase. You can pay £40,000 to a 'personal motion picture company', eDv, to make a full length feature film about you and your family – and Dutch speakers can even create their own soap opera by posting text, photos and videos on Netherlands based website, www.soapshow.com. A recent television programme called *Britain's Biggest Spenders* featured Lisa Voice, former girlfriend of the singer Billy Fury who is spending $50 million on a film about her life story. Her grand plans envisage that Renee Zellwegger will play her part, and Johnny Depp will star as Fury.

There is also an increase in the disturbing tendency to sensationalize death through international media coverage and global outpourings of emotion. In some parts of the world it is commonplace for mourners at funerals to express their grief very publicly, though Princess Diana's funeral marked a significant change in the way that public feelings were openly expressed and displayed in the UK. The media's obsession with disaster scenarios and celebrity status has led to a glut of universal grieving - all of it available for digital viewing and much of it showing little discernment as to the nature of the tragedy, whether it be 9/11, the tsunami, the death of footballer George Best or the murdered My Space member, Anna Svidersky. Such expressions somehow seem only to devalue the remembrance of the countless servicemen the world over who died for their countries during two world wars.

Nonetheless I predict that we will gradually see more genuine public manifestations of our desire to be remembered forever, not just for the sake of it, but to honour and allow others to reflect upon our worthwhile achievements and contributions to mankind. None of us worthwhile achievements and contributions to mankind. None of us wishes to be forgotten, as Joyce Vincent was. Nor do we want our memories to slip away when we die.

Robert Holden points out *"Interestingly, obituaries rarely mention the deceased's up-market properties, their top of the range sports cars, their upper echelon china and cutlery. What is mentioned is how well they lived, how loved they were, how much they gave and the difference they made. Obituaries are full of value measurements."*

Fortunately, if my research, wisdom and instinct are anything to go by, we are at the beginning of a major shift towards a renewed interest in family history, social responsibility, local networks, community-based interest groups and the value of life as determined by our ultimate mortality ... or immortality.

PART ONE

LIFE TRENDS

Predicting the Future

The Reality:

Forecasting trends and predicting what is likely to happen in the future is not at all easy. To be clear, a prediction is a forecast of something that might happen in the future, whilst a trend is a general tendency or direction - a fad, craze or fashion. So trend forecasting is about predicting the potential future course of things. Sometimes these are short-term, as with fashion trends in colour, textile, fabric and design and sometimes they are longer-term – such as environmental change, or trends in demographics and society.

Trend forecasting isn't an exact science – it's based on a cocktail of objective research, intuition and experience. In part it analyses the scientific evidence for such things as environmental changes or changes in medicine or new technology. At the other extreme it is more instinctive using gut feelings, even telepathy. So, why is trend forecasting necessary?

Trend forecasting, often termed futurology, can be used by individuals and organisations to create a better future for themselves. It helps us to understand possible future developments, to make better decisions, develop worthwhile goals and become more aware of the risks and opportunities ahead. In this way we can predict future lifestyles; business people can anticipate profitable new markets and innovations, investors can be prepared to participate in new technologies, teachers and parents can help ensure that children are properly prepared for the world they'll inherit, students can plan out careers and policy makers can make provision for a successful future. Ultimately, we all shape the future, because the ideas we buy into are the only ones that will succeed.

And why is the art of predicting the future so difficult? Massachusetts Institute of Technology professor Noam Chomsky says, *"Perhaps the most plausible prediction is that any prediction about serious matters is likely to be off the mark except by accident."*

In his book *A Brief History of Tomorrow*, Jonathan Margolis points out that *"Even brilliant people who should know better have demonstrated a penchant for short-sighted prediction, especially in their own field."* He refers to some amusing examples – The Nobel Prize-winning physicist, Ernest Rutherford, the founder of nuclear physics who once declared that talk of nuclear power was "moonshine". Britain's Astronomer Royal, Sir Harold Spencer Jones, who dismissed the idea of space flight as "bunk" in 1957 a couple of weeks before the Soviet Union launched Sputnik 1 - and Thomas J Watson, the former CEO of IBM, who, in the late 1940s said, *"I think there is a world market for maybe five computers."*

Futurologists have been around for many centuries. In 16th century France, Nostradamus produced seven volumes of The Future Events of the Entire World. He predicted that the human race would survive until 1999 when *"from the sky there will come a great king of terror."* This and almost all of Nostradamus's prophecies have proved to be wrong. Add to this the fact that the emergence of science over superstition has massively altered the way in which people view the future prospects for humanity, and it is surprising that so many people today still take heed of his predictions and are happy to re-interpret them over and over again! But this is probably because such prophecies help people to ponder over, rather than carefully analyse, catastrophic events affecting our fellow human beings. The way that the media sensationalizes terrorist acts, natural disasters and tragic accidents also encourages public anxiety and makes us search for an answer to the question 'Why?'

An example of this is the BBC news report in 2005 that a new flu pandemic (a hybrid of avian/bird flu) could happen at any time and kill up to 150 million people. United Nations Official, Dr Nabarro, said "*It's like a combination of global warming and HIV/Aids ten times faster than it's running at the moment.*" For now, though, it all remains hypothetical. In fact, in an article in the British Medical Journal, dated 15th April 2006, the government's chief scientific adviser David King, is quoted as saying that the chances of the virus mutating into a form that could spread between humans are "very low" and that it is "totally misleading" to say that such a mutation is inevitable.

In his book, *The Politics of Fear*, sociologist, Frank Furedi, suggests that the more secure a society is - in terms of health, wealth and political stability - the more likely it is to fixate on theoretical menaces. In turn, the more obsessed we become with keeping safe, the more insecure we become, he says, "*because safety becomes this elusive quest you never achieve. Even if you never leave the house, you can always slip in the bathtub.*"

Most of the far-fetched scientific predictions of the post-war period were based on real knowledge, "*albeit tinged with intuitive genius*" says Margolis. In 1945, Arthur C Clarke made one of the most famous and accurate futuristic predictions of all time when he proposed an orbiting communications satellite system to spread radio and television signals all over the world.

The entertainment industry and science fiction films have been responsible for some of the more wacky predictions of recent decades. From *Dick Tracy* to *Thunderbirds*, from *Star Trek* and *Lost in Space* to *the Jetsons*, you'll find all sorts of unusual and inventive glimpses of a futuristic world – some of it wonderfully improbable and some remarkably true to life. A relatively recent film called *The Island* features Scarlett Johansson and Ewan McGregor as clones on the run from their biological twins, for whom they were created to provide spare body parts.

From the 1960s onwards futurologists have tended to look increasingly towards societal and environmental concerns. In the 'hippy' days there was a fashionable return to Malthus – the fear of a huge population explosion, the exhaustion of natural resources and general environmental disaster. Today, the world's population is around six billion – and the prediction for 2050 is between nine and ten billion. But in 1964 Jon Fremlin a British physicist writing in the *New Scientist* speculated that by the beginning of the 23rd century there would be 400 billion people – and by the 29th century, 60,000 trillion – a million times today's population. He predicted that people would have to spend their lives lying prone and eating recycled human bodies in cubicles in 2,000 storey buildings spread over both the land and the former seas. He claimed that eventually the population's combined body heat would cause the extinction of the human race.

Another preoccupation of recent decades has been the length of the working day. In 1966, a spokesman for General Motors, talking on a BBC documentary said *"People will start to go to work at about the age of 25. Six month vacations will not be out of the question."* Whilst Alvin Toffler in his cult bestseller *Future Shock*, predicted that all this free time would cause us to require leisure counsellors. Many of us are still looking forward to this! Much more recently predictions about the future have focused on topics such as global warming, artificial intelligence, life-extension and new forms of fuel and transportation. The focus is no longer on technological advancement but on improvements in environmental, medical and spiritual conditions.

Futurology has more to do with possibilities than improbabilities. In 2005 an article in the *Sunday Telegraph* entitled '*Stairway to Heaven*' noted that "*The future of space could be an elevator to lift astronauts and rockets into orbit.*" This is not some hare-brained professor's mad fantasy. On the contrary, "*NASA is putting up funds and trials are about to begin.*" Scientists believe that a material known as carbon nanotubes could be bound together to make a ribbon rather than a cable three-feet across but just half the width of a pencil and thousands of miles long. This would be able to support 50,000 times its own mass and, when secured to a satellite counter-weight, could be used to carry people and materials into orbit.

What once sounded like science fiction now features in the news as perfectly plausible if it isn't rapidly superseded by something even more advanced. There is huge competition between originators and manufacturers of products and services to come up with the most saleable version of an invention. Research led me to the Japanese company, Fujitsu which has created a workable technology that will turn a bulky newspaper into a single sheet of thin plastic. *The Times* says "*It's patented 'e-paper', a wafer thin film of plastic that can slip easily into a handbag or briefcase will turn each new page at the push of a button.*" It is predicted that although the handheld screen has failed to take off in a serious way this product will be everywhere from advertising hoardings to fridge doors very soon, as evidenced by Massive Inc's dynamic billboards.

The potential for a world where e-media predominates is sensationally depicted in a video clip produced by Florida's Museum of Media History – see www.epic.lightover.com. They predict a world where the press ceases to exist because all the information is "in the hands of the people." The video suggests that computers will be able to write news stories and customise each offering to the individual user – EPIC; the Evolving Personalised Information Construct will filter, order and deliver information from the people to the people. Everyone will get a share of the revenue from the system, proportional to their contribution and the traditional newspaper will become a print-only newsletter for the elite and the elderly. To some EPIC will represent a summary of the world that is "*deeper, broader and more nuanced than anything we have seen to date*" but to others it will be just "*a collection of trivia, much of it untrue – narrow, shallow and sensational.*" It is we who will choose the product but it will be free of either democratic or journalistic ethics.

The idea of computers creating the news is made more feasible when we consider that Scientists have already developed the world's first 'telepathic typewriter' – a device that literally allows users to make a mental note. A prototype being developed by Germany's Fraunhofer Institute uses brain sensors to detect what a user wants to write and could give paralysed people the chance to communicate more easily – as well as revolutionising office life for millions. Scientists in Germany have also come up with a computer program that can recognise early signs of stress through high-tech sensors linked to a computer. Microphones and cameras will pick up voice patterns and facial expressions and this information will be fed into the computer. The Department of

Computing at Imperial College in London is also working on eye-tracking technology, enabling computers to be controlled by eye movements, rather than a mouse or a keyboard. This means that computers of the future could monitor and react to the mood of their operator – which could rule out shouting at your computer screen or slamming down your mouse in frustration! There are other potential applications for this technology such as installing sensors on car dashboards to warn drivers when they're falling asleep. A rather more alarming proposition is that such a device could also be used to enable fighter pilots to aim missiles correctly, by simply looking at the target. Meanwhile, experts in Japan are working on mobile phones that can lip-read. According to *New Scientist* Magazine a new range of 3G phones will recognise words through electrical signals sent by mouth muscles. The signals will then be turned into speech, text messages and even emails.

A cash-free society has been widely predicted - a new system called Paybox allows users to settle bills by mobile phone. Started in Germany in 2000, it now has almost a million members who use Paybox to settle accounts in approved restaurants, hotels, taxi cabs and cinemas. The need to rummage around for cash is averted by simply adding the client's mobile phone number to the bill. An automated answer-service calls the customer back and asks for payment to be confirmed. An SMS message is then sent as receipt of payment. I predict that this is the way forward, especially when wrist-watch-sized mobile phones are likely to be available in the near future. Once we have micro-chips implanted under our skin, already being trialled by some supermarkets, there will be no requirement for money at all.

An even scarier prognosis for some is the potential future advance of artificial intelligence. Major futurists in this area include Ray Kurzweil author of *The Age of Spiritual Machines* and Hans Moravec, who predicts that machines will attain human levels of intelligence by the year 2040. By 2050 he believes that robots will have surpassed us all, displacing workers and causing massive, unprecedented unemployment. Intelligent robots will effectively become our evolutionary heirs. Hiroshi Ishiguro, professor at Osaka University's department of adaptive machine systems has created the world's most lifelike robot to date. ReplieeQ2 seems to breathe, can speak and flutter her eyelashes. Unfortunately robots are still a long way from humans. Repliee was modelled on the Japanese television news presenter, Ayako Fujii and she is so stunningly attractive that it is easy to see how 77% of people who met her at the 2005 World Expo failed to notice that she was a robot! *"We can learn and build a better relationship between robots and humans"*, says Ishiguro. Nanotechnology is also being developed whereby machines (or more likely software embedded in our houses) would be so small as to enable us to manufacture everything we need from atoms at home. So we are likely to have much more time to spend on leisure pursuits, perhaps cerebral interests, or even spiritual pastimes.

Another important recent trend has been the increasing focus on spiritual awareness. In their autumn/winter 2004 trend briefing, the Future Laboratory refer to this as being *"A decade of re-enlightenment."* They claim that whilst we are richer, we are not happier but we are more culturally and spiritually aware.

Carmen Harra, a gifted psychic and author of *Everyday Karma – How to Change your Life by Changing your Karma* says *"A shift in the consciousness of humanity is happening as we leave the place of "I believe in God" to the place of "I know God." We will come to evolve spiritually, to know our creator and be in tune with our creator, so that our existence is a reflection of this divine perfection, rather than the evil qualities of human nature.*" In her book written in 2002, Harra predicts that "*We have entered a different era and will be in transition until 2033. After years of change and transition, we will enter an era of peace... There will be a new world over night – new laws, new inventions and discoveries and new science.*"

Harra predicts that we will start to use more than ten per cent of the brain and will eventually communicate telepathically as well as being able to communicate regularly with our loved ones on the other side. We will have one monetary system all over the world using codes – there will be enough money for everyone and we will eventually live in a time when our accomplishments are not measured by money. No one person will have power, there will be a 'collective consciousness'. There will be one world religion, acknowledging one God, a new understanding and a new prophet to show us the way. Harra's optimistic vision of the future concludes with the prediction that "*Man will erase evil from the earth within 150 years.*" In the meantime, should we not ask whether one of the most significant developments this century will be to discover the essence of human consciousness? This is difficult enough to define precisely, let alone quantify.

Dr Rapaille Clotaire, cultural psychologist and the inspiration behind Chrysler's novel design of PT Cruiser uses a regression technique to tap into the sub-conscious thoughts of his subjects' brains for research purposes. He believes that each individual receives a psychological imprint when they have a meaningful experience of something for the first time – whether it's smelling coffee, having their hair washed or getting into a car. The shared experience of similar imprints between people of the same backgrounds is what creates archetypes, which vary from nation to nation, forming a collective consciousness. So if you're British you see the world through British glasses, if you're American through American glasses, and so on. A similar principle is mooted by Ketan Patel ex head of global trends at Goldman Sachs. In his book, *The Master Strategist,* Patel claims that the West has traditionally focused on breaking external boundaries – in space, biology, computing – whilst Eastern thought has looked inside through meditation, metaphysics and lucid dreams. He claims that the 'master strategist' must combine both approaches.

Meanwhile, Dr Rapaille isolates the codes of the associations within each collective unconscious for sales purposes – for instance he was commissioned by Kraft to isolate the code for cheese. For the French, cheese is "alive" something sensuous which should be touched in order to assess its quality and texture. A French advert may therefore show a woman handling cheese and leaving fingerprints in the surface. But for Americans the same imagery is horrifying. They want their cheese to be "dead" – pasteurised, sealed in plastic and kept in the "morgue" of the fridge!

There is much food for thought in every prediction. The realm of the futurologist encompasses historical knowledge, experience, intuition, research, careful consideration, scientific calculation, foresight and frequently a sixth sense. Predictions come and go – you have probably heard about the likelihood of future generations being born with strong thumbs for texting and game boys – 'texter's thumb', or maybe more recently, 'iPod finger'... of the idea of a 'smart key' that can be used for everything – to get into your house, to activate your car, to use the machines at your gym, to get money from an ATM, perhaps even the key to your DNA. Like most predictions some may come true but many will be superseded by ideas, innovations and inventions that are, as yet, unidentified. Damien Broderick in his book *The Spike: How our Lives are Being Transformed by Rapidly Advancing Technologies* (2002) provides evidence to support the fact that if you put progress on a chart and draw the last 300,000 years of mankind's progress in transport speed increases you'll see a flat line until you get to the furthest edge of the graph – then a near vertical spike. Recent research has proved that the rate of technological innovation has, in fact, slowed down over the past few decades.

However, there *has* been a revolution in digital communications - and the use of the Internet now affects every area of our lives. Despite this, I believe that the changes that have had the most marked and traumatic effects on our lives in recent decades have had much more to do with cultural, social, economic and even biological transformation than technological improvement. Even with the spectre of global warming looming my view is that it is likely to be the speed at which life is conducted on a day-to-day basis, the variety of choices available to us and the overwhelming number of things we perceive we are expected to pack into our increasingly pressurised lives that will influence us most, both as a society and as individuals, in years to come.

The Disposable Lifestyle of a Virtual World

Dealing with Rapid Cultural Change:

Speed dating, Internet porn, pod-casts, web-based gambling, online auctions, designer handbags and sunglasses, mobiles, reality TV, celebrity magazines, plastic surgery, doggie boutiques, virtual dieting, outsourcing, downloading, texting, grazing, retail therapy, psychic guidance, wonder drugs, launch parties, the next big thing, x is the new y, express spas, themed restaurants, concierge services, one-stop shopping, disposable nappies, self-tanning, personal styling . You've heard it all before – so what's new?

Key elements of our lives have become as transient as the words that describe them. There is a constant need for re-invention: Just look at the timeframe in which houses, offices, hotels and restaurants are bought/sold/refurbished. Some people may even undergo several complete overhauls of their face and body during their lifetime. In an ever faster and more competitive marketplace, advertisers and branding professionals spin out terminology for ever more short-lived products and services. With so much more to fit into our lives it's hardly surprising that drugs are being developed to eliminate tiredness, thereby eliminating the need for sleep.

In *Dictionary of the Future*, Faith Popcorn and Adam Hanft provide a fascinating preview of some of the words and terms that capture tomorrow's innovations and forces of change. Terms such as: 'DNA'd' – when you're dumped from a relationship because your genes don't match; 'Mannies' – male nannies, who are growing in number; then there are 'Yoghurt Cities' with 'active cultures', providing a broad range of interests to those who live there and 'Free-Range

Children' who are raised without much structure in their lives. 'Eternity Leave' is time off work to be with someone who is dying and 'Ego Auditors' are to help executives keep their sense of perspective. 'Wristicuffs' is fighting it out with email and a 'SHUV' is an accident caused by an SUV (sports utility vehicle). Whilst these books make amusing reading they generally have a very short shelf life. And short shelf life syndrome is spreading fast…With the cult of celebrity upon us everyone's 15 minutes of fame has to be acknowledged, even if it's just for that 15 minutes. And sooner or later, we'll have streets named after characters we don't even know, let alone remember, from soaps and reality TV shows aired on inconsequential digital channels that spring up and close down by the week. I recently visited Microzine, a man's shop in Islington that changes every month - like a magazine. The idea of giving the customer what they don't know they want is now crucial to winning new business. Trends in fashion point towards the emergence of the disposable wardrobe. If you can buy a whole outfit including the shoes and bag from Top Shop, Primark or River Island, why bother to pay over the odds for the designer version? You can probably afford to keep up to date with the latest looks on a weekly basis – maybe daily. In any case, the clothes may fall to bits if you wear them for more than a week. And how long till everyone is on to this and is stocking their wardrobe with disposable items? You could even mix them in with a few carefully chosen designer or vintage items purchased from E-Bay – and when you've had enough of these you can simply put them up for sale again. With so much choice and so much change, people get bored all too quickly!

Military research laboratories have begun to develop a fabric whose colour and pattern can change, allowing the wearer to blend into any background, like a chameleon. This fabric would potentially be made of a flexible computer screen. The same technology can also make clothes glitter more than sequins or jewels. Spanish designer Manuel Torres has developed a spray-on cotton fabric that can be applied as a light mist or a thick layer. It can be as tight as a second skin or left loose. Swimmers of the future could spray on just enough cloth to protect their modesty and spray on bandages could provide instant covering for wounds says Suzanne Lee in her book, *Fashioning the Future*. Researchers at the London College of Fashion are working on technology that would allow garments to be woven to order in nylon or cotton their shape determined by a computer. They hope to combine this technology with 3-D body-scanning equipment allowing everyone to wear made to measure clothes.

The future promises 'smart' clothes – nanotechnology-based utilitarian clothing that will monitor cardiac health, muffle smells, radiate heat, download podcasts, change texture or shape and tell your washing machine which cycle to use. Over a decade ago US forces were issued with combat uniforms that had been treated with an insecticide called permethrin that repelled mosquitoes and other bugs. The product was so successful, you can now buy treated gardening aprons and Tommy Hilfiger has even designed a line of golf shirts and polo shirts treated with the insecticide.

An article in the *Sunday Telegraph* outlined how "*garments that advertise your sexual availability and display your changing emotions in kaleidoscopic colour like the skin of a cuttlefish*" are coming soon. Firms like Sony, Bosch, DuPont, Motorola and Thyssen are all working on projects to develop 'intelligent' fabrics with micro-chips sewn in. An interactive fashion and smart textile design company based in Spitalfields in London called CuteCircuit already produces a dress called the Mystique – it starts above the knee and automatically gets longer as the day goes on so *"by the evening you look like a Hollywood star"*, explains the designer.

Hand in hand with this ability to metamorphose at your every whim, it seems to me there is a genuine paranoia about actually being real. Even babies (soon to be cloned) are being sold on the Internet. An advertisement in a Sunday magazine supplement entitled *"May God Bless You, Little Grace"* showed a picture of what appeared to be a real live baby – for sale! But no, this was a "So Truly Real ™" "Early Arrivals Doll" with "Real Touch ™" vinyl skin and a tiny disposable diaper. To behold this extraordinary gift go to www.bradford.co.uk where you can not only see Grace, but also some of her baby friends. Alternatively, you might like to visit www.eccky.com, a multi-player concept that allows two people to create a virtual baby, add it to their MSN buddy list and guide it through its childhood and teens. The look and characteristics of the child are based on the unique DNA of its parents which is derived from a quiz the couple takes before conception. The parents then have 6 days (equivalent to 18 years in Eccky time) to raise their Eccky into a healthy and happy 18 year old. The instant messenger service, MSN messenger is used as the communication tool to bring about this transformation.

The massive trend towards a virtual existence may well be one of the defining features of our age. In their December 2004 trend-briefing, www.trendwatching.com wrote about "Masters of the Youniverse" – consumers who wish to be in charge of their own destiny by creating their own comfort zone, or universe. Internet games such as Habbo Hotel (www.habbo.com), which has 50 million members around the world, enables users to do just this. According to Mediaedge:cia, "*Gamers all over the world are looking for the same thing: escapism – the opportunity to participate in an alternate reality. Within this alternate reality, fundamental human desires are satisfied – the drive to explore, with the promise of reward.*" In computer games, you can create an alternate being or you can simulate your real life (RL) identity by creating a personalised avatar (a graphic image to represent your persona in the virtual world). You can even custom-design your own hang-out, or "crib" and import your buddy list to join you. www.secondlife.com, is another 3-D virtual world built and owned by its residents. Secondlife currently has over 300,000 members around the world, but it is growing exponentially largely due to the transferability of is virtual currency into hard US$. Reuters has recently announced it is to set up a virtual news agency on the site.

Edward Castronova, Associate Professor at the Department of Telecommunications at Indiana University studies these online environments and claims that "*synthetic worlds threaten the lines we have drawn between fantasy and reality.*" Google is said to be working on a site that combines Google Earth with Google Sketchup. www.metaverseroadmap.org analyses the growth of this phenomenon, which is called 'metaversing'. A metaverse is "*Where video meets the Web; When virtual worlds meet geospatial maps of the planet; When simulations get real and life and business go virtual; When your avatar becomes your blog, your desktop, and your online agent.*" Castronova says that, as a parent and a gamer, he is "*both excited and concerned about these developments.*" His concerns may surface again over a new site launched in the summer of 2006 – www.naughtyamericathegame.com, an x-rated space where avatars can sexually explore like never before.

According to the *New York Times* in 2005, more than 100 million people world-wide log on every month to play interactive computer games. With such enormous numbers of gamers involved, advertisers have also identified the benefits of Youniversal branding, or 'virtual product placement' as it has become known – from adding their real world logos to their virtual counterparts (eg cars, beauty products etc) to setting up their own gaming websites: Coke Studios (www.mycoke.com) has more than 8 million users alone.

There is a definite trend towards making money out of the unnecessary from a population that seems to have more money than sense. In a world where Tim Berners-Lee, the the originator of the Internet and a physicist from CERN in Geneva, sought no monetary reward for his contribution to society - enter that highly lucrative proposition, the Crazy Frog!

In 1997 Daniel Malmedahl, a Swedish 17 year old recorded his impersonation of sounds made by a child imitating an engine which he sent to his friends' computers and they put it onto the Internet because it sounded funny. In 2001 this was used by Insanity Test in an online joke. It was picked up by Erik Wernquist a designer of 3D graphics in 2002. He created an animated frog character which he called 'The Annoying Thing' on his company's website. The ringtone was merely a by-product of this. In 2004 a worker at Jamba! a German ringtone company spotted the Annoying Thing's popularity and bought the rights. Then Jamba! (part of Jamster!) was purchased by VeriSign, a Nasdaq listed US corporation with a capitalisation of more than $4.3 billion.

The Crazy Frog rapidly became the number one ringtone and a record that was released by the frog became No.1 in the popular music charts. This was probably the result of a clever pairing of the internet with mobile phones, combined with the vital market for teenagers texting each other. Remarkably this happened without any traditional media involvement nor were any shops involved - such is the power of digital communication.

What we are being given now is a huge variety of options of new and often totally dispensable products and services in every area of our lives. Just look at the turnaround of restaurants - how many are newly opened up… and closed down? How many styles of décor are available and how many types of food? Hardly surprising that the "restaurant of the year" should be Heston Blumenthal's "Fat Duck" at Bray – offering a menu based on molecular and physical gastronomy. The 16 course tasting menu at £97.50 per head includes *'Nitro green tea and lime mousse, Snail Porridge, Roast foie gras with Almond fluid gel, cherry and chamomile, Smoked bacon-and-egg ice-cream and Leather, oak and tobacco chocolates'* amongst other delicacies. Possibly ideal for that 'once only' visit before you venture forth onto the next new culinary experience? There's even talk of a new microwave oven that will spare those under time-pressure the effort of reading cooking instructions. Just scan in the barcode on the side of the product and the oven selects the correct cooking temperature.

And after endless hours of troubleshooting on www.pchell.com to try to find out how to get rid of your computer virus, after downloading countless upgrades to your system, after finding that your brand new Blackberry is already out of date, why don't we just go back to using paper and sending let-ters? Emails are, after all, as disposable as the rest of our modern throwaway lives – and they can be deleted at the click of a button. Writing letters we don't run the risk of hackers infiltrating our computers and stealing our personal information such as bank account/credit card details, or worse still – our identity!

Scientists conducting research at London University discovered "infomania" fixation. Essentially, over-reliance on techno modes of communication – mobiles, texting and e-mail is making us stupid. Sending and receiving texts and emails apparently temporarily knocks ten points off your IQ (as opposed to smoking a joint which reduces the score by only four points.) The effect on concentration is so bad that researchers say that those who constantly stop what they are doing to respond to a text or e-mail are suffering a similar effect on the brain as that which comes from losing a night's sleep.

Advertising agencies have even recognised that traditional forms of advertising are too long to hold the attention of young people who might simultaneously send a text, email a photograph and download a piece of music in the time it takes to watch a TV advertisement. CPA, or Continual Partial Attention, as it has become known, has led to the increased use of viral marketing campaigns, especially via the Internet. One of the most popular has been Burger King's banal yet entertaining www.subservientchicken.com . And with Youniversal branding advertisers are able to introduce virtual goods and services that would take years to develop and produce in the real world.

Meantime this information overload finds people logging on at night to do their Internet banking and online shopping as they're too busy keeping up with the demands of modern technology during the day. There are even new drugs like Modafinil that will enable us to structure our sleep to suit our lifestyles – sleep and wakefulness will eventually become available on demand. US-based pharmaceutical company, Cortex, is developing another new drug, CX717 that helps brains and bodies to recover without sleep. Professor Russell Roster, a circadian biologist at Imperial College, London envisages a world where it might become routine for people to be active 22 hours a day and sleep two.

There's a general consensus that we're already living in an uncaring society where everyone has to do everything for themselves – phone messages are automated, fast food outlets are self-service, a 'find it for yourself, or fuck off and die' mentality prevails. Definitely not a place for the old, or the incapable. Rates of depression are soaring as communities break down and many who cannot turn to traditional support systems such as religion or the extended family are turning to 'comfort behaviours', otherwise known as addictions! Dr Robert Lefever of the Promis Recovery Centre groups such compulsive behaviours into clusters: the hedonistic cluster, which includes alcohol, drugs, caffeine, sex and gambling; the eating disorders cluster, which includes shopping, work, cosmetic surgery, sunbeds and exercise and the relationship cluster which includes compulsive helping and love addiction.

The lack of meaning and purpose in our lives is exacerbated by the fact that disposability is fashionable. Like most things nowadays, we love to have a 'get out' clause. Responsibility is a virtue that too many of us shy away from. I have noticed that everyone wants to be an intermediary: no one wants to be directly involved. Ideas are wanted to make money for us – not to help us work together. Look at the increase in numbers of so called concessions in department stores. Shops such as Dover Street Market in London are based on the principle of making a profit not just from selling other people's goods but from renting the space to them in the first place. Venture capitalists and TV programmes such as *Dragons' Den* and *The Apprentice* have spawned funds specifically to feed off other people's ideas – and increasing numbers of companies make a living this way. Some people make a full time occupation from finding the cheapest solution to everything – and what about all those 'no win, no fee' solicitors, computer repairmen and the like. Then there's the growth of agents who can assist us to sell our possessions and "collectibles" on Ebay or www.podserve.co.uk who will upload entire music collections onto iPods and hard drives – taking a fee or a cut of the profit for themselves in the process.

Even being responsible for who we are is considered to be undesirable – look at all the dating sites with spoof members – just how many of us are secretly married, posted a photo that was taken ten years ago or made up something about ourselves because it sounded interesting or seemed like cheap, harmless fun at the time? We want to be protected from others who aren't like us yet we want to be individual at the same time.. maybe there's so much choice out there that we are afraid to just 'be'? To quote J Robert Lennon from *Mailman* "*People…want to be protected from hearing, even having to look at other people who aren't like them, but at the same time want to assert their individuality, want to 'be themselves', want to wear their beliefs like a pair of baggy pants and dump them the second they go out of style.*"

ESSENTIALS FOR REAL LIFE - THE BACKLASH:

So when will having too much freedom and too much choice become tiresome? Which products and services are truly essential? Food of course is one of them along with water, heating and shelter. And then there's hairdressing if we don't all want to look like trolls, and clothes – though there's always a chance that naturism will be popularised (not just by dirty old uncles). Accountants and solicitors seem to survive, whatever happens to the rest of us. Fitness of body and mind are useful for a long and healthy life, so maybe sports and leisure are up there somewhere - and perhaps sex comes into this category?

Sleeping is also useful so I guess that beds will always be around in whatever form the fashion of the day dictates. Pets are apparently good for our emotional wellbeing too though hardly essential. Travel and communication are pretty important. But can't we walk…and talk??? Do we really need Homechoice TV? Do we need agents to help us buy and sell stuff on Ebay because there's so much on there it befuddles our already overwrought brains? What is it that we genuinely need – and how much of this stuff is totally superfluous?

If you have the money and not the time there are many concierge services who will make your hectic life much more manageable for you. There's Coutts World Concierge and Assistance Service, Quintessentially, and all manner of boutique time-saving services – you can let them take the hassle out of your life. Having said that you will still need to be able to afford these services, tell them what you want them to accomplish and ensure that everything is how or where it should be in order for them to be able to achieve the desired result on your behalf. Like most things in life – it's a function of 'garbage in, garbage out!'

Perhaps the information overload and the enormous range of opportunities available to you are already confusing enough to make you want to go back to the so-called 'good life'? Carl Honore's *In Praise of Slow* uncovers a worldwide movement that is challenging "the cult of speed." The leading proponent of deceleration is Carlo Petrini, the Italian founder of Slow Food, headquartered in the Piedmontese city of Bra – an international movement dedicated to the civilized notion that what we eat should be cultivated, cooked and consumed at a relaxed pace. Honore describes how Pro-slow groups are springing up all over the place *"Among these are Japan's Sloth Club, the US-based Long Now Foundation and Europe's Society for the Deceleration of Time."* He goes on to outline how *"In the workplace, millions are pushing for – and winning – a better balance between work and life. In the bedroom, people are discovering the joy of slow sex, through tantra and other forms of erotic deceleration."* The notion that slower is better underlies the boom in exercise regimes from yoga to Tai Chi – and alternative medicines – from herbalism to homeopathy – that take a gentle, holistic approach to the body. Cities everywhere are revamping the urban landscape to encourage people to drive less and walk more. It is also likely that global warming will necessitate such changes.

I predict that there will eventually be a much greater backlash away from the 'throwaway' society towards a more human existence. It will become evident to more and more people that mass consumption of material goods and the idolisation of designer brands is not guaranteed to provide happiness. Human responsibility and human touches will not only be appreciated but also valued appropriately – and potentially even cherished. I don't think it at all likely that we will become cyborgs – we're too easily irritated by technology for that. Eventually we might find it easier to focus on living our lives for the moment rather than watching others live theirs on Big Brother. We might even learn to love our lines and wrinkles – and see ourselves for what we really are – the most amazingly beautiful, extraordinarily complex, creations of flesh, bones, organs and souls that ever existed on our planet.

The human touch will have a very significant comeback in response to the feelings of isolation and remoteness caused by the age of information. People will start to write letters to each other as a reaction against the overwhelming volume of emails sent and received. More specialist stationery shops will appear to provide a greater variety of notepaper and cards. Websites such as www.letterlover.net will even help you to compose your missive. How refreshing it is to receive a letter, to hold and experience the weight of the paper, to see a card that reflects the personality of the sender through their handwriting or choice of design. Sending letters gets you noticed - send your resumé by email and you may be treated as spam. People will also start socialising again in small groups as an antidote to online chat forums. There will definitely be an element of snobbishness involved - and those who consider themselves to be most cultured and refined, or have more disposable income to pay for uniqueness, will be the most particular about personal service and individuality. We are already seeing a return to the employment of household staff such as dog-walkers, cleaners, ironers, people to do the school run, mobile car-washers and so on.

Time and space will also be recognised as a new premium currency. Post-technological revolution many people no longer define their lives by where they work and are taking the opportunity to move out of towns to the countryside. This shift from urban to rural living has become known as 'greenshifting'. Where we once enjoyed BBC sitcom *The Good Life* extolling the delights of self-sufficiency in leafy suburban Surrey we now have a new TV show – *The Green Green Grass* about Boycie moving from inner city Peckham to the rolling hills of Shropshire. Even sleep has become a luxury activity. New York based MetroNaps rents out futuristic sleep pods by the hour in airports around the world – the first London pod is due to open soon, charging customers £10 for 20 minutes sleep.

The tourist industry is booming – in particular spa and activity holidays. We want to rest and pamper ourselves but we don't want to slow down so much that we're bored. Recreational breaks are becoming extremely popular – especially as they are considered a healthy and worthwhile change from sitting on the beach sipping cocktails. Cycling for charity, trips to Cuba, China or Mexico, Sports, Fitness and Wellness weeks at Club La Santa in Lanzarote, or Le Sport in St Lucia; kitesurfing, windsurfing and just plain surfing with companies such as www.itimeexpereince.com or luxury spas and yoga/meditation vacations in Thailand, Sri Lanka, Ibiza and the Turks& Caicos islands…a great deal of money is disposed of as we spend cherished time in beautiful places, relaxing and sharing a premium lifestyle experience with like-minded friends and relatives!

Along with holidays another pastime for like-minded people with plenty of time on their hands will be 'specific interest groups'. These include book, cinema and supper clubs, debating societies and discussion groups, arts clubs, exclusive and luxury goods clubs such as The Ferrari Owners' Club, Damon Hill's P1 prestige and performance car club and private jet charter syndicates. Personal interest clubs are definitely back in vogue and likely to proliferate all over the place. Apparently the rather antiquated and sedate pastime of knitting is one of the latest activities to spawn clubby get-togethers. As it happens our rediscovery of all things old sits rather nicely alongside our rediscovery of all things new. Our enormous thirst for education seems somehow linked to the urgent quest for knowledge brought about by the digital age. Whilst Radio 4 listeners are eagerly awaiting the time when podcasts of *The Archers* will be available and *Daily Telegraph* readers are enjoying online *Sudoku,* there is suddenly a huge demand for retro furniture and the press seems to be gradually realising that we should probably give more credit to and appreciate the appeal of restaurants that have been around for more than a couple of weeks.

In the meantime, Dr June McNicholas, a prominent research psychologist informs us that pets can act as a great stress reliever *"They provide time out of the rat race,"* she says, *"And that may be the only time you are not having demands on you."* More than a decade ago, a landmark Australian study found that pet owners displayed significantly lower blood pressure, cholesterol and triglyceride (fat) levels than those without. There's even a charity called Pets As Therapy (see www.petsastherapy.org) which provides therapeutic visits to hospitals, hospices, nursing and care homes, special needs schools and a variety of other venues by volunteers with their own friendly, temperament tested and vaccinated dogs and cats. Today there are currently around 3,500 active PAT visiting dogs and ninety cats at work in the UK. Every week these friendly dogs and cats give more than 10,000 people, both young and old, the pleasure and chance to cuddle and talk to them. The bedsides that are visited each year number a staggering half a million.

Dr June McNicholas believes that pets also give people the opportunity to have 'risk free' relationships. Maybe this helps to explain why pets have lately become the *de rigueur* accessory for many celebrities. Having pets as our most trusted companions gives us the option to renege on our responsibilities to our fellow human beings. The sad truth is that it's become not only acceptable but also fashionable to be totally selfish. The outcome of a disposable lifestyle where there is plenty of choice for everyone and no one cares much for anyone else is that there's always the option to move onto the next new thing if you get fed up with what you already have. For the young in particular, the options available - from downloading the latest music to buying new friends online - abound. The problem with this 'must have now' culture is that constantly replacing the old with the new has influenced (some would say severely damaged) our value judgements. A few decades ago we were shocked if women had children outside wedlock, divorce was rare, and drug-related gun crime was something we thought was confined to New York's Harlem, or South-Central Los Angeles. A disturbing trend is that the line between the rights we, as individuals expect, and our responsibility to each other has somehow become strangely blurred.

Rights vs Responsibilities

Coping with a 'New Morality':

The main problem we face is one of human rights. Not the right to feed the starving or deal with the relative poverty that is endemic in large parts of the world. More about how expanded freedom of choice and the extended scope and proliferation of individual rights is eroding our responsibility to each other and to society in general.

The dreadful cliché (that is so overused by government ministers and officials that I find myself clenching my teeth together in embarrassment every time I hear it mentioned) is of trying to 'create a level playing field'. In their efforts to make everyone equal, the resulting social landscape is more likely to resemble a pot-holed, torso-strewn minefield where only those who can either afford to opt out of the system or are savvy enough to work it to their advantage survive.

Political correctness is furthering the growth of an underclass of people expecting rights regardless of responsibility. The right to have a child whether or not one is in or out of a responsible relationship; the right to own a property whether or not one has a regular income; the right to live in the country of one's choice whether or not one has a job; the right to medical care whether or not one is addicted to an illegal substance; the right to social benefits to top up the black economy and hence pay for items such as cars, digital TVs, DVD players, iPods, trashy celebrity obsessed magazines and training shoes (whether or not they are stolen), these are all presumed rights. A new form of 'anti-traditionalism' is emerging where not only taxes, but the whole system and structure of society is biased against the wealthier classes and, increasingly, against those in regular employment, the middle classes and the older members of the population. Reverse discrimination will ultimately result in services (such as the police force, hospitals and schools) being largely staffed by ethnic minorities and the less able. Sub-standard levels of service and responsibility will be become acceptable and criminals condoned and included in our dysfunctional, anti-traditionalist world.

We are already experiencing the effects of too much choice in every area of our lives. What is the point of having this freedom if we never think to ask what it is for? Bel Mooney, writing in *The Mail on Sunday* points to the 24 hour drinking culture as an example of something the Government is foisting upon us in the name of choice. "*No matter that senior doctors and police have combined to beg a rethink. No matter that binge drinking threatens the health of a whole generation, as well as public safety...many people want to be able to drink all day and all night and, in the name of 'consumer demand' they will be given what they want.*"

Even youngsters who think they are doing the right thing by furthering their education are rapidly becoming an "*iPod generation – Insecure, Pressured, Overtaxed and Debt-ridden*" – according to a study by Reform, the think tank. While previous generations enjoyed higher education funded by the taxpayer young people today face university tuition fees and a declining return in the salary advantage they will get from their degrees.

Some of these graduates will drop out and become dependent upon the state; others will simply remain dependent upon their parents. These youngsters are becoming increasingly incapable of handling their own lives, of preparing for adulthood and learning the skills necessary to leave the parental home – a problem exacerbated by so called 'helicopter mums' who 'hover' over every aspect of their children's existence prolonging adolescence well into adulthood. According to the most recent figures from the UK's Office of National Statistics 56% of men (980,000) aged 20-24 and 37% of women (650,000) were still living with their parents after completing their college education – an increase of 50% in ten years. One of the largest groups of dependents is lone unmarried mothers who have outnumbered divorced single mothers for more than a decade. According to the UK Office of National Statistics the number of married couple families fell by 4% (0.5 million) between 1996 and 2004 (see below, 1996 in black). This decline occurred despite an overall increase of 3% in the total number of families. At the same time, the number of cohabiting couple families increased by over 50% to 2.2 million, while the number of lone-mother families increased by 12% to 2.3 million. By 2004, nearly nine out of ten lone-parents were lone-mothers.

Michael Buerk sees this as part of the gender revolution but also points out that "*This is not independence. The reality for many women is swapping dependencies – relying on the state for welfare or childcare, rather than the father.*" He adds that

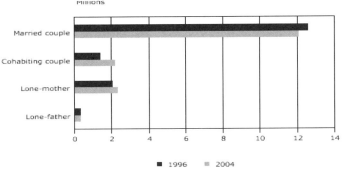

ALL FAMILIES: BY FAMILY TYPE, UK OFFICE OF NATIONAL STATISTICS

although the gender revolution may be long overdue and good for us all, "*if it squeezes fathers out of families it will have consequences we all live to regret.*"

Meanwhile, I note that under-aged teens are being advised 'how to be good at sex.' In early 2005 the fpa, formerly the Family Planning Association, published a booklet called *Love, Sex and Relationships* – aimed at thirteen to sixteen year-olds. And this despite the legal age of consent being sixteen and the spiralling rate of sexually transmitted infections and the highest rates of under-sixteen conception in Europe. The booklet includes sections on oral sex, orgasms, contraception, body image (including plastic surgery procedures such as breast enlargement), sexual orientation, homophobia, sexual attraction and dealing with rejection. The philosopher, Roger Scruton, recently wrote "*When sex becomes a commodity, the most important sanctuary of human ideals becomes a market. That is what has happened in the past few decades, and is the root fact of postmodern culture.*"

Nowadays children have their own rights and are entitled to their every demand and desire being seriously considered by their elders at home and at school. Teachers are taught not to offend children by teaching them to spell correctly – instead they are requested politely to refrain from using too much red ink to indicate spelling errors. Green ink might not appear so offensive and too many corrections may give the impression that the children are inadequate and so undermine their sense of self-esteem. So the kids just assume they can spell how they like, that learning doesn't matter, that in fact they can do what they want: They'll probably spend the time that would have been used to correct their spellings insulting the teacher and fighting with their classmates. But are we going to introduce more discipline and rules or simply encourage a potentially anarchistic, ill-educated underclass to determine how the rest of us live our lives (ie paying taxes and contributing to the black economy to fund their reality TV lifestyle?)

Shaun Bailey, who grew up in a single parent family on a North Kensington, London council estate recently described in the *Sunday Times* "*how pop culture and liberal politics have created a feral generation hooked on drugs, crime and violence*" as depicted in the film, *Kidulthood*. His recipe for stopping youngsters becoming criminals includes being taught that money and goods must be earned, not taken – and shielding young people from commercial exploitation and the celebrity culture. He concludes that "*Poor people don't need all this liberalism. They need direction. Everybody talks about 'my rights' – but there is some point when your behaviour needs to be balanced by your duty to the community. The working class look to rules... Take away the rules and they are left in limbo. So they form their own: the kind that are driven by pop economics and lead to crime.*"

Even the children of those affluent and educated enough to know better are losing their way. In her book *The Pampered Child Syndrome*, Maggie Mamen says "*We live in a child-centred society where children's wants and demands are increasingly given priority over marital or family harmony, financial considerations, parental sanity, common courtesy, quiet enjoyment, respect and common sense.*" She describes how well intentioned parents are catering for their children's every whim and actively avoiding, even resisting, their parental responsibility to say no, to set limits, engender a sense of responsibility and teach morals, values, the importance of family and community. "*Children are not learning active or creative problem-solving strategies, or how to be resilient and responsible, or to build up a range of internal resources to manage stress, loss, failure or disappointment. As a result, many are chronically miserable, angry and anxious (more than 40,000 children and adolescents in Britain are currently using anti-depressants).When they don't get what they want they are violent,verbally abusive or unwilling to see how their behaviour affects others. And when they finally enter the real world, they lack the tools necessary to survive."*

Pampered Child Syndrome is often a result of parents feeling guilty about working long hours – they want to make up for any unhappiness they have caused their children. Many parents believe that competition is negative, they even change the rules of games so that no one loses.They believe that expressing anger is destructive and that voices should never be raised at home. They are then surprised when their children struggle at school, when their behaviour becomes anti-social and when they lose interest in anything except for smoking dope and drinking alcohol. There is no doubt that parents need to reclaim authority and responsibility for running the family as quickly as possible. If children are given the freedom to do exactly as they please then they will do just that; irrespective of what is morally, legally or considerately right or wrong. What's more, the so called 'nanny state' has initiated demands for anti-smacking legislation, now the norm in most European countries. Such legislation will make it harder for parents to discipline even the most unruly children and in any case, children can always sue their parents if they aren't happy with the way they are being treated!

Bel Mooney says *"Like 'freedom', democracy is a fine word, but it is threatened by a dumbed-down culture of disrespect. Figures of authority – teachers, police, church leaders, politicians – are not given the respect they once commanded and this spirals down so that toddlers witness their parents being abusive and threatening to nurses, teachers and anyone else who dares to say something they don't want to hear."* Frank Furedi writing in *The Times* says *"People no longer unquestioningly do as they are told and those who claim authority without having earned it are rightly treated with derision and contempt. There is much to welcome in this – but at the same time no society can work unless some forms of authority are respected."* Bel Mooney talks of *"aggressive materialism"*– which deludes us into thinking we have the right to own virtually anything we want, breeding selfishness and self-importance. *"We should ask ourselves if we want to live in a society that does harm, is unworthy and has lost the ability to make moral judgements."* In the words of Margaret Thatcher *"We want a society where people are free to make choices, to make mistakes, to be generous and compassionate. This is what we mean by a moral society; not a society where the state is responsible for everything and no one is responsible for the state."*

In terms of a moral society, a new authoritarianism has certainly emerged where lifestyle gurus tell us what to do – from life-coaches, to makeover gurus, super-nannies and dietary experts - we are being constantly told how to behave, dress, decorate our homes, exercise, relax, eat and live our lives. The messages they are giving us are in a way similar to old-fashioned family values though unfortunately they tend to lead us to distrust our own instincts. As Frank Furedi says *"The collapse of authority for respect hasn't freed us – it's just made us slaves to a new set of masters.... The political class has shifted its deference to the authority of celebrity. Like most of us, our leaders are happy to listen to Bob Geldof moralising about how to save Africans or Jamie Oliver instructing us how to rescue our children from obesity."* And it's not just celebrity culture that has replaced authority. Post 9/11 and the second Gulf War, the threat of terrorism has made our lives much more regulated. In the UK, the State is subtly becoming more authoritarian by using our fear of terrorist attacks as a weapon of control, attempting both to introduce ID cards and to suspend *habeas corpus* to detain terrorist suspects for up to 90 days without charge or trial (although, after a vote in the House of Commons this was limited to a maximum of 28 days). In other subtle ways, the UK Government is turning to 'emotional literacy' as a potential panacea to its disaffected youth. *The Sunday Telegraph* has reported that "*Parents increasingly can no longer be trusted to teach qualities such as self-worth, restraint, friendliness, empathy and resilience to their children so schools must assume the burden.*" They are proposing worry boxes, where pupils write down their anxieties and post them into a box to be considered later in a class discussion, friendship tokens, feeling fans, mood music and emotional barometers. The National Union of Teachers' commented that "*This concentration on schools adds to some parents' assumptions that their children are someone else's responsibility.*"

The USA has already experienced a major backlash against declining morals. This has expressed itself in a falling teenage birth rate and an increasing adherence by many young people to the belief that sex before marriage or simply teenage sex, is not such a wonderfully liberating thing after all. A recent article in *The Observer* magazine picked up on the way in which this trend had filtered through to the UK: entitled *Down with Everything – Meet the New Puritans*, it interviewed a girl whose dislikes included "binge drinking, debt and possessions." Whilst her likes included "*being in control and getting good grades.*"

As society has become more immoral ethics are becoming big business and "ethics committees" are popping up all over the place. But in a world of so many changes and so much choice we still seem rather confused about which morals to uphold and which to offload. According to a report by the Social Affairs Unit think tank, traditional morality has been replaced by 'new morality' which means that if you're not harming anyone, then anything you choose to do is fine; and if you are harming someone that's when you're actually doing something wrong. So apparently we should all do what feels best for us – ie recreational drugs are okay so long as they're not taken in front of the children; infidelity is okay if you are unhappy in a relationship or you need to get revenge; lying is okay if you want to sell your house, apply for a job or have a day off work. Shane Watson says "*In this fuzzy, grey hinterland you can get away with anything providing you don't get caught, or you can turn it into a joke.*"

It's hardly surprising with all these variants on what is right and wrong, on what's important and what isn't that in the adult world there's a growing sense of confusion and loneliness leading to a focus upon all things spiritual. To quote Shane Watson "*There are now so many means of distancing ourselves from the ordinary business of life, it's harder than ever to feel sure of who we are and what our place is in the world.*" This sense of being lost is being translated into a huge upsurge in spirituality. People are seeking retreat, sanctuary, even monasticism in reaction. Every religion will experience a renewed appeal – and interfaith churches and gatherings will become particularly popular. The Interfaith Seminary www.interfaithseminary.org.uk for example offers to train ministers and spiritual counsellors for the new millennium, giving participants the chance to "*Explore the heart of the world's primary faiths and mystic traditions, substantially deepen your personal spiritual life and practice, refine your capacity to be a loving presence in the world and deepen your authentic purpose and way to serve.*" I also predict that meditation will become a major growth area, since it combines individual introspection and a (usually) spiritual purpose.

There will almost certainly be a marked growth in the number of shared, tailor-made communities around the world focusing on ecological and environmental concerns. People will group together to educate their children as a result of what they see to be the failure of the state to fulfil the role. They will grow their own food and share houses and transport (all of which will become increasingly necessary as supplies of fuel gradually become exhausted). The major difference between these groups and those living in communes set up in the past such as those created during the hippy era in the 1960s and 70s, is that they can all be globally linked via the Internet. In effect, the Internet will provide a global context for local communities.

People the world over have been shocked by recent terrorist atrocities in New York, Bali, Egypt and London, as well as by natural disasters such as the tsunami, hurricane Katrina, the famine in Niger and the earthquake in Pakistan. But such events have actually brought people of vastly different countries, races and religions closer together – and again Internet communication has been the great faciltator. The bomb attacks in London in July 2005 have awakened the British nation to its cultural diversity. According to the 2001 census one in four Londoners is born abroad. London is home to 200 ethnic communities from more than 62 countries, speaking 307 languages. With immigrants making up one third of the 52 fatalities in the July bombings Londoners defiantly declared with some justice that "*an attack on London is an attack on the world.*" This process of unification through diversity is one of the positive things to emerge from new social and demographic trends brought about by rapid global change, combined with modern digital communications.

Sharing a common spiritual belief system is another way of taking advantage of the new social glue that binds us as a result of our increased technological closeness to each other. Bel Mooney, who has presented a series on Radio 4 called *Devout Sceptics* for the past 10 years says "*even in atheists there is a deep need for meaning: to know we are on this Earth for a purpose.*" Although an agnostic, Mooney shares with people of all religions "*a belief in compassion – the ability to see sacredness in every single human being and a willingness to take care of the vulnerable. Such moral values are perverted by terrorists and threatened by selfish materialism. But they need to be fought for – as the only hope we have.*"

I feel we also have another hope in learning to value our lives by appreciating that we are only on the earth for a limited amount of time. In this way we'll be more motivated to ensure that the contribution we make to life and our planet is as helpful to our fellow men as it is worthwhile and rewarding to ourselves. We can also learn from the experiences and mistakes of others who have now departed from this world. It is somewhat surprising given the relatively recent legacy of two World Wars that we continue to fight, country against country, in battles over our resources or our beliefs. We are currently in a position where leading world powers are products of their industrial and financial achievement. However the old world order is changing as rapid technological advancement creates new rivalries between those striving for economic dominance.

The Competitive Edge

Winning in a Changing Global Marketplace:

Here in Britain it may sometimes seem that our workforce has become a disposable part of the global 'winner takes all' economy. A new flat world is being created thanks to the fibre optics revolution. A recent article in *The Mail on Sunday* starts *"First it was directory enquires, phone banking and even medical records – now GCSE marking has become the latest service to be farmed out to India."* 'Personal off-shoring' is the new term to describe how people save money by delivering a service digitally from wherever is the cheapest place in the world. Online homework tutoring, building websites and even the most sophisticated software development: the cheapest deals may be found by going offshore be it Estonia, Pakistan, Gujurat or Gdansk.

Thomas L Friedman describes what he calls the *"flattening of the world"* as *"the most important force shaping global economics and politics in the early 21st century."* Friedman describes how we are now in the process of *"connecting all the knowledge pools in the world together…we are on the cusp of an incredible era of new innovation…Only 30 years ago, if you had a choice of being born a B student in Boston, or a genius in Bangalore or Beijing, you would probably have chosen Boston… but not any more…For decades you had to leave India to be a professional. Now you can plug into the world from India. You don't have to go to Yale to work for Goldman Sachs!"* Microsoft's Asia centre is already their most productive research team in the world – The enormous intensity of competition it takes to win a job there is explained by the fact that *"in China, when you are one in a million, there are 1,300 just like you."* Friedman concludes, *"When I was growing up, my parents used to say to me 'Tom, finish your dinner, people in China are starving'. But now I tell my daugh-*

ters 'Girls, finish your homework – people in China and India are starving for your jobs.'"

There has always been healthy competition but in business today I sense that competition is becoming ever more intense. One of the main areas of recent rapid growth is business networking groups. The concept of personal branding, self-promotion and competitive marketing to thrust oneself into the limelight and up the corporate, or these days entrepreneurial, ladder is everywhere. And it's an open question as to who reaches the top and who lands at the bottom of the heap. Keith Ferrazzi's book *Never Eat Alone* is based on the principle of "becoming a member of the club." As Ferrazzi says *"I came to believe that in some very specific ways life, like golf, is a game, and that the people who know the rules, and know them well, play it best and succeed. And the rule in life that has unprecedented power is that the individual who knows the right people, for the right reasons, and utilizes the power of these relationships, can become a member of the 'club'"*…. Even if they started out, like Ferrazzi, as a caddie!

Networking groups such as Ecademy (www.ecademy.com) promote the ethos of open and honest business amongst a community of online "friends" - people such as Richard Duvall, Chief Executive of Zopa who describes his product as part of *"The Individual Revolution.…We are all changing – suddenly, radically and permanently. The consumer revolution of the last 50 years is giving way to the Individual Revolution of the next 20. People who used to define themselves by what they consume – by the brands they wear, by the cars they drive and by the consumer electronics they own – now define themselves by their self-expression – by who they are, by how they lead their lives and what they care about. Technology is enabling the change. We are at the start of the age of domesticating and humanising information technology. The internet, personal computer, mobile phone, gaming console and iPod are putting the individual in control – helping people to do things that once only professionals were able to do."* Mr Duvall was the co-creator of Egg 'the world's largest stand-alone digital bank' and his latest creation, Zopa is 'the first lending AND borrowing exchange'. What a brilliant idea, taking money on both sides of the deal – ingenious!

Yet all this competition for the latest idea, all this clamour for funding or for market attention is entrepreneurship gone overboard. Indeed the Ecademy website may to some represent a severe case of information overload. To me this is just the beginning of a trend that is already transforming the world order. New parts of the world will gain prominence as the Internet opens up international markets to players across the globe. The CIA's World Factbook estimates that in 2004 there were 604,111,719 Internet users world wide – including 206,032,067 in the European Union and 159,000,000 in the United States of America.

The UK's Office of National Statistics shows how Internet access has risen in the UK alone (see next page). Over half (55%) of households in Great Britain could access the Internet from home in July 2005. The new flat world is going to result in a totally new social geography for all of us. I predict that parts of what we formerly called the Third World – both demographically younger and technologically more aware - will become the Second World. The old First World will start to run out of money due to huge levels of debt incurred in part by paying off the debt of former Third World economies and supporting both an ever-growing social underclass and an ageing population. The old First World will suffer the burden of a lack of savings and pension provision. There

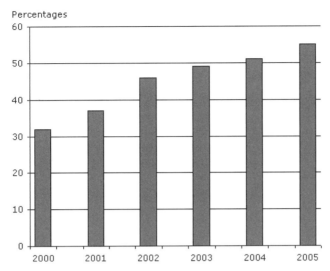

Percentages

UK HOUSEHOLDS WITH ACCESS TO THE INTERNET, JULY 2005. 12.9 MILLION TOTAL

will be crises caused by competition in energy pricing and supply as well as other products and services with strong international demand.

A new First World will eventually emerge where - thanks to a new set of 'community values' disseminated via the Internet - goods, services and benefits to society will be much more equally distributed. Money will ultimately have far less significance and may well eventually be replaced by concerns for ecological and social harmony. Although there is current-ly what has been termed a 'digital divide' between those with access to home computers and high powered broadband connections, and those obliged to use Internet cafes or unable to pay for Internet use, I foresee that there will eventually be a chance for all of us to be provided with access to the Internet which will be seen as a basic human right. Other basic rights will of course include some form of shelter, a supply of water and a source of power. But before we reach this blissful place, there is going to be plenty of discord.

It is likely that the economic war between countries vying for competitive advantage to access limited resources will intensify. Only when we discover alternative energy sources and/or are prepared to tolerate a significant humanitarian shift in our international relations will we embrace peace on our planet. Getting there may well bring us to the brink of destruction but, hey, we know that the going gets tough before we reach enlightenment! The battleground created by economic forces is not the only one we will find ourselves faced with. It is also probable that the battle of the sexes will become more and more challenging, as the combined factors of social, cultural and medical change lead us to re-assess our relationships with each other.

Wars of the future?

Re-assessing Relationships in a Time of Dramatic Social Change

In the early 1970's, a book called *Woman in the Year 2000* predicted that contraceptives would be available free at the Post Office (I'm still waiting!), that conception would take place in laboratories with gestation in artificial wombs and the gender of babies would be ordered in advance. Homosexuality would be totally accepted - and marriage would be a contractual matter involving lawyers to look after the long term interests of both partners. One story in the book tells of a girl born into a world where male violence on television has been banned. At school she learns that girls are expected to fight whilst boys are always crying.

Not quite yet but the huge and relatively recent transformation in female rights and behaviour in the Western world has caused many to say that this will be 'the female century'. Over the past few decades we have experienced the most extraordinary transformation in the male/female societal balance. Unlike former times, we are now in a place where women are treated as equals to men in the workplace and where both men and women are probably more likely to meet their future partner on the Internet than at a family gathering or a social event.

Michael Buerk, defending controversial claims made on TV is quoted from *The Mail on Sunday* as saying *"We suddenly live in a women's world, played according to women's rules. Women's supposed virtues are everywhere triumphant in the contest of values. To be a woman and, therefore, by definition caring, nurturing, co-operative, pacific, adaptable and in touch with your emotions, is the acceptable side of being human. Being male, in any traditional sense, is unacceptable. Traditional male virtues aren't just unfashionable; they are dysfunctional. Stoicism, reticence, courage and single-mindedness are signs of emotional immaturity these days. Strength is mere brutishness now it is no longer necessary. Young men seem to have two choices: to go with the flow and become 'new men' ie quasi women, or to play up to the current critique of masculinity and be lads, behaving badly and enforcing the new stereotype."*

Women these days are generally in competition with men in the workplace – and that has spilled over into their personal lives too. Men's loss of power in the office environment and at home has led them to seek solace in lap-dancing bars or online sex and dating sites where there is no need for any commitment to the female of the species. Women's distrust of men has been exacerbated by men's abuse of women to satisfy their sexual desires. A typical male comment might be *"I've always wanted a harem, but I can't afford it!"* (not that men haven't always wanted to have lots of partners to spread their seed).

In the distant past men focused on hunting and protecting their women and children, whereas women were caring and nurturing. Our basic instincts haven't changed that much since we were cavemen and women – they are still based on survival and protection. It's just that society has changed so dramatically we have all become horribly confused. I heard someone mention the other day that masculine energy is about being in control whilst feminine energy is about letting go. This struck an awkward chord with me but, truth to tell, the question of who's in control is probably the key to relationship problems. Many high-powered affluent women are dissatisfied with the new breed of male. As they seek perfection in all aspects of their lives, they are looking for a man who has everything – good looks, impeccable manners, excellent grooming, superior social skills, high earning capacity, a brain the size of a small planet - someone who is an awesome lover, is honest, generous, kind, compassionate, witty and will also be the perfect father to their children. Increasingly demanding requirements of the dating market have resulted in a glut of niche websites such as www.lovehorse.co.uk for lovers of equestrian pursuits; www.loveyoga.com (self explanatory) and www.loveair.co.uk for cabin crews! The new breed of 'überwoman' is so certain that her ideal man is out there somewhere and is so determined to track him down that she usually remains single until it is too late to become a mother. A new problem for such women is that men often use online dating services to meet women for one night stands and casual relationships so that women, who are more earnest – and honest - in their approach to relationships, have been left feeling very let down. Likewise, many divorces are the result of female dissatisfaction with their spouse's inability to live up to their decidedly unrealistic notion of what a partner should offer.

I have observed that the competition against men is growing and gaining momentum as more and more women are promoting and profiting from their advantages – including their sexuality – in ever-cleverer ways. From the crude propositions of the Thai porn industry to the highly sophisticated lifestyle of international jet-set call girls, women the world over are taking advantage of men's ultimate weakness to achieve domination, rather than subservience. Meanwhile, the new breed of überwoman is using her power and influence to keep her men under control. From house husbands and male *au pairs* to doting fathers, professional escorts, walkers and sperm donors – the überwoman certainly knows how to get the best use out of her men. Males are unlikely to be in danger of becoming redundant but with falling levels of fertility and the increasing use of sperm banks they will be in greater demand for their reproductive usefulness and, of course, they could always come in handy for a spot of DIY!

Men are reacting to their increasing feeling of being superfluous by spending more time alone, in the office, at the computer, together in bars – mainly away from women. What's more, they are becoming more like women in their emotional responses, attitudes and consumer preferences. A new company, Metro-Sexual (www.metro-sexual.co.uk) offers an online one stop shop for all new man's needs, whilst several operators have recently opened private members' clubs and salons devoted to men's pampering. According to Michael Buerk "*Manliness is out. Androgyny is in. Men have been turned into "metrosexuals," preening, moisturiser addicts.*" However, there is also said to be (due to a trend apparently instigated by male porn sites) an increasing interest in brawny, hairy and muscular "real men".

Therapist Paula Hall says that the most common new issue affecting men is their low libido and other sexual disorders. Rather than work pressure, being overweight, the use of antidepressants or alcohol, a theory often advanced to explain dwindling sex within relationships is that many men are caught up in a caveman/caring paradox that didn't bother their fathers. Sex therapist Marianne Brandon says "*Women encourage men to become more loving and caring, but when men respond and develop their feminine sides, they find it harder to take the initiative sexually.*"

Nirpal Dhaliwal says that in response to feminism and the rise of the ambitious, independent and successful 'alpha' female, "*British men have become weak, gelatinous omega males, unwilling to even admit let alone express their manliness in case they are made to sleep on the couch for daring to have the backbone.*" He adds that "*In her determined climb up the ladder, the alpha female has no time for men with minds of their own: husbands and boyfriends are merely support staff, assisting her career by providing constant reassurance and an emollient, stress-free domestic life.*" Dhaliwal also notices a difference between men of different races and believes that white men have possibly cultivated effeteness to try to mark themselves out as being more civilised, whereas black and Asian males have cultivated an image of more robust masculinity, as represented in their increasingly macho music.

So are men really becoming more like women? A BBC programme, *Secrets of the Sexes* investigated 'Brain Sex' – an exploration of the psychological differences between men and women. It asked for example why women like relationships and men like facts – i.e. girls like people and boys like things? They concluded that the reason why many men find making emotional contact difficult and are less proficient at linguistic things and more able at visuo-spatial tasks was due to their genetic make-up and in particular, to the level of testosterone affecting the organisation of the brain. However whilst the rule could be generally applied that men had more male brains due to more testosterone and women had more female minds due to less testosterone each person has their own unique mix of male versus female brain. Some women could have much better visuo-spatial skills and inferior language skills if they had a slightly higher level of testosterone. This explains why some women make excellent airline pilots and others don't!

Women have already learned to take the initiative: Younger women are already "doing it for themselves", socialising in "packs," attending hen nights and, in addition to the old-established women's clubs with their stuffy image, new girls' only clubs such as www.rudegirls.net provide titillating male-free entertainment. A recent article in *Time Out* recommended *Mamma Irene's Love Bar* as the best on the women-only circuit, claiming, "*Girls get to have all the fun.*" We are likely to see a time when vast numbers of disaffected divorcees, unable to find suitably responsible male partners, will team up to help each other out. On the flip side you'd imagine that someone as rich and thin as Kate Moss could live her life in any way that she desired. However, Shane Watson writing in the *Sunday Times* says that the reaction to her cocaine scandal proves that the rock'n'roll lifestyle is only fine if you are a man. She says "*Kate is branded a dirty slut because she has broken the first commandment of female acceptance and tried to play by men's rules.*" She says it's okay if you're Robert Downey Jr, the Gallagher brothers, Keith Richards, Pete Doherty or one of countless wife-beating, violent footballers: your hell-raising will be celebrated by adoring fans. "*Any woman who has ever tried to keep up with the boys knows that she flouts the prescribed behaviour of her sex at her peril. Marianne Faithfull was denounced by the Pope for living like a Rolling Stone, whereas Mick Jagger cruised towards a knighthood. And although 30 years have passed since she was hung out to dry, nothing has changed.*" Or has it?

In their characteristic way, men are retaliating by turning to PUAs (Pick-Up-Artists) for advice on techniques to seduce women. PUA 'lairs' such as London's Leicester Square are the hotspots for this kind of activity – where tourists and hen parties in particular, become unwitting targets for preying men. Neil Strauss, author of *The Game*, explains how Internet based seduction gurus have emerged over the past decade due to a growing uncertainty among men about how to deal with modern women. Many feel they are just too ugly or clumsy to get a date without help. Maybe these guys should just resort to selling their sperm and retreating to the lap-dancing bars? Another alternative is to buy a virtual girfriend. Hong Kong company, Artificial Life, have developed a computer game available on 3-G mobile phones that enables the subscriber to date an animated girfriend called Vivienne. The product of voice synthesis, streaming video and text messages, Vivienne is available for a monthly fee of $6. On top of the cost of text messages to and from Vivienne, men are charged extra to buy flowers and gifts for their girlfriend and each girl behaves differently according to the amount of money spent on her. Vivienne can translate six languages (doubling as a translator for travellers) and converse on 35,000 topics from philosophy to movies. Boyfriends can buy their way towards their first virtual kiss, or even marriage. But whilst Vivienne is fairly prudish and not allowed to bare her midriff for fear of offending Muslim boyfriends, there are other sites where one can find girlfriends such as Hottie 2, a web-based game for new style men with more carnal interests.

And as for old-style man ...*Sorry, you **are** the weakest link, goodbye!* Now it's more acceptable to be in touch with our emotions women are becoming all too aware of men's faults. It has already been reported that women are becoming problematically assertive. A survey by advertising agency, JWT, found that 23% of men and 22% of women could imagine a time when men became the weaker sex and that 61% of men felt that their status had deteriorated in relation to women. Many of the men interviewed said that they were tired of feeling belittled especially in advertising. One in two men felt less sure of himself than he used to: 71% were confused about how women wanted to be treated. India Knight writing in the *Sunday Times* about whether women should be sexually aggressive, or the gentler gender says "*It's a minefield, not least because the* *women themselves have become muddled about the answers. So nobody seems very happy.*"

Paul Nathanson and Katherine Young describe the modern contempt for men as *misandry*, the opposite of misogyny in their book *Spreading Misandry: The Teaching of Contempt for Men in Popular Culture.* They say that "*Misandry has become so deeply embedded in our culture that few people – including men – even recognise it.*" Maybe, but the few would have quickly realised had they watched any of the recent BBC series called *Bring Your Husband to Heel* – Its premise was to use a dog trainer to help women control the men they married! Nathanson and Young point out that "*Misogyny has been studied and taken seriously for decades. Political pressure has eliminated or at least hidden a great deal of misogyny. No pressure has been used to eliminate or hide misandry. On the contrary, pressure used against misogyny has directly or indirectly exacerbated it. As a result the world view of our society has become increasingly focused on the needs and problems of women and the evils and inadequacies of men.*" They go on to say that attacking the identity of any group of human beings is "*an extremely dangerous experiment.*"

There's a strong possibility of a backlash against feminism – perhaps we'll see more and more men converting to pro-polygamy religions such as Islam, or Mormonism? Apparently there has already been a marked increase in the use of *burqas* (traditional Muslim headdresses) in Britain. As well as concealing the bruises from beatings used to force women into arranged marriages or simply show them their place, this form of dress perpetuates the 'puritanical' existence of its Muslim wearers and acts as a constant reminder that their male counterparts retain control. However it might be, statistically, we are still living in a man's world. When the Sex Discrimination Act was introduced 30 years ago, the job market in the UK was dominated by men. There were 15.4 million men in work and only 9.5 million women. Now there are still 15.4 million men in work, but the number of women has shot up to 13.2 million. The shift from manufacturing to a service-based economy has favoured women and attitudes to women working - as opposed to staying at home to look after the children - have been transformed. Nevertheless, women do not occupy the same proportion of senior positions as men and they trail men financially. Women who work full-time earn 18% less than men and women part-timers 40% less. The differences are as wide as they were 30 years ago. Only 17 executive directors of FTSE 100 companies are female, as opposed to 400 who are male. However the author Fay Weldon points out that "*Women rule the media and education…And this is very serious because they influence how people think and behave.*" However, she also describes a "*lost generation*" of women, who because of the economic necessity to work "*find themselves starved of love, sex, children and leisure … They are overworked, stressed, tired and exhausted.*"

My prognosis is that an almighty battle of the sexes is looming on the horizon. This will not be a war of the battlefield, using arms - nor will it be a war of the board-room, involving share-ownership – but it will be a full blown war of relationships, centring on procreation and men's ability to satisfy women's ever increasing demands. We'll start to see many more women with portfolio relationships with lots of men in tow. Basically, a woman will have one man as a lover, another as a cook, one will be a sperm donor, one her confidante and best friend, another for intellectual discussions, a different man will be her dresser (maybe a gay man could become her combined dresser/confidante …) More men will simply be around – in fact, she might have a whole team of men to keep her lifestyle operational and functioning up to just the sort of high standards she expects.

Despite the increasing demands of a relationship, getting a new partner in the future is going to be less hassle. It will probably only be a short time before mobile/text-dating becomes much akin to telepathy – We'll have microchips implanted in us so we can sense who is or isn't compatible. The senses and powers of reasoning relayed by the microchips will be carefully engineered to replicate real human feelings, biorhythms, personality characteristics and experiential behaviour patterns. Potential employers will be able to identify us in this way and our friends will be able to tell what we are feeling. At least then we'll be able to abrogate the responsibility for failed relationships and jobs that don't work out - we can simply place the blame upon flaws in our embedded microchips… The fact of the matter is that many more of us will simply be happy to live alone anyway. As cult shows such as *Friends* and *Sex in The City* have shown, it's fashionable to be single. In fact with the current trends towards self-development there's a tendency to want to focus on educating oneself before entering into any relationship. But where exactly will a culture of 'singledom' lead us? This is examined next.

Baby Blues

The Future of Marriage and Family Life

A report published in October 2005 by the Institute of Public Policy Research states that around ten per cent of 25-44 year olds now live alone compared with just two per cent in 1973. It calculates that by 2021 thirty five per cent of all households in Britain will contain just one person. In addition to divorce and bereavement, the aspirational desire for singledom was one of the key factors creating this trend – and this aspirational desire to be single is particularly marked in the case of young, middle-class women. There are now huge numbers of females living alone in cities in the 'developed world' who can't seem to find the right partner. They have become feisty and independent but are still needy. Many young women have come to feel that a loving relationship is in itself a physiological remedy to the human condition, comparable to taking medication. Contrast this with the period just after the First World War when there were huge numbers of unmarried women who seemingly managed to cope without a mate!

When they do finally get married even American brides are rejecting the vow to love 'till death do us part' in favour of more cautious promises such as one to stay together 'for as long as our marriage shall serve the common good'. A survey by professional wedding planners estimates only one couple in five (of this year's 2.6 million weddings) will stick to the traditional wedding script. The rest will either update the wedding vows or create them from scratch often lacing them with private jokes. People tend to be more realistic about marriage these days … Especially if they are onto their second or third marriage. When the actors Brad Pitt and Jennifer Aniston married in 2000 she promised to make his favourite banana milkshake while he vowed to "split the difference" over the temperature they wanted in their home. After their separation Pitt said that he still considered the marriage a "*Total success…That is five more years than I made it with anyone else*," he said. Will Smith, the actor, recently revealed that when he married Jada Pinkett in 1997 "*Our vows did not promise to forsake all others*." The vow that was made was that "*You will never hear that I did something after the fact*" so one spouse will ask the other "*Look I need to have sex with somebody, please approve it*."

As most of us who have tied the knot are aware the cold truth is that marriage is hard work. Just look at the short-lived attempts of those in the media spotlight such as Ulrika Jonsson. Whilst most people take their jobs seriously (along it seems with most money-making activities) there appears to be a distinct lack of responsibility for valuing and respecting relationships – and sometimes the offspring that result! If we are to maintain the contract of marriage, I'd suggest a new set of vows more relevant to the reality of modern relationships – for instance:

Treat your partner, as you would expect to be treated;

Be open and honest;

Set aside time for intimacy;

Care equally for offspring;

Be respectful of each others' differences;

Above all, be realistic in your relationship…

Meantime, in the absence of marriage and children many women are simply turning to their pets for the missing maternal love. Lizzie Spender in *Wild Horse Diaries* says she always assumed she would have a child, but she simply left it too late. "*A lot of friends my age fell into the 1970's trap of juggling careers…* *this current generation are a million times better at juggling the careers and the children and telling the husbands to change the nappies.*" She says she can't think of anyone she would have had a child with … When they were both about 35, Angelica Huston said to her "*You do realise that anyone who has a child now has to be prepared to bring the child up on their own.*" Lizzie says that thought had never occurred to her before – She thought you had to "*find the person you wanted to spend the rest of your life with and you were going to have children only with that person.*" She adds, "*I think for those of us who don't have children, it's great to have stepchildren and god-children, but maybe we can treat ourselves to animals, be it a dog, or a cat…. or a horse.*" Lizzie is totally besotted with horses, "*The relationship with animals is somewhere to give your maternal love.*"

On the flip-side, Steve Friedman reviewing *Bastard on the Couch* recounts a modern bachelor's nightmares… "*Now that a woman can have a baby by herself, and can make more money than I do, and now that there are few sabre-toothed tigers, my historically most salient attractive selling points – brawn, ferocious cunning, massive earning power - and the ability to protect and provide for and otherwise nurture my helpless and pregnant wife and our mewling offspring – don't matter so much. Nowadays, it's a sellers market, and I'm the hapless buyer.*" He says, "*A woman who shuns marriage and believes she's fine alone frightens me. I'm not fine alone. Why should she be?*" A recent *Sunday Times* article I read featured Lori Gottlieb. Her approach to men and childbearing reminded me very much of a close friend of mine who had recently purchased the sperm for her beautiful child over the Internet – She is now pregnant with her second child using the same sperm. And another friend of a friend, a former banker at Goldman Sachs, who decided her boyfriend wasn't committed enough to be the father of her child and opted to go down the sperm bank route. Though this does of course seem to beg the question, exactly how committed is a sperm donor?!

Lori Gottlieb recounted how she learnt about an organisation called *Single Mothers by Choice* at the end of 2003 when she was 36 and almost two years into a relationship with a handsome, intelligent man. Their personalities had been clashing and she was looking for a perfect i.e. unreal mate. *Single Mothers by Choice* was a group for women like her who want to have children, but don't want to shack up with the wrong guy to do so. *"Its members — mostly attractive, smart, successful thirtysomethings — subscribe to the 'somebody isn't always better than nobody' theory of marriage."* Sperm donor profiles read like online dating profiles but with the addition of health histories and education results (see www.cryobank.com). Another American firm, www.hellobaby.com offers women the chance to hear the voice of donors through a 20-minute interview and audio CD answering a range of business school type interview questions. Even Gottlieb's take on this first step towards the creation of designer babies was that *"Without the emotional context, finding a donor seemed less like the intimate act of choosing my child's father and more like buying a car."*

Gottlieb describes herself as an *"X-generation slacker who rebelled against baby boomer careerists. Unlike women a decade or two older, we took it for granted we could do anything we wanted — which explains why a lot of us became paralysed by indecision. With so many choices in jobs, relationships, geography, we didn't know when it was time to pick something permanent…sometimes we forget that if you don't choose anything, eventually you're left with nothing."* Lori Gottlieb saw the whole process of finding the perfect genetic father as a *"silver lining. By bypassing the uncontrollable world of romance, I was able to choose a man to father my child who might be complete-*

ly out of my league in the real world. Instead of marrying a schlubby but lovable man and thinking, I hope our kid doesn't get his crooked nose or bad eyesight or thin hair, I could pick from cold, hard DNA."

Professor Steve Jones, author of *Y: The Descent of Men*, points out that every time a man has sex he has enough sperm to fertilise every woman in Europe. *"So the question is: Why are there so many men... Why isn't there just one? Why do you need so many when you've got a deep freeze?"* In the UK alone, around 82,000 single women in their 30s have a baby without a partner, almost double the figure from a decade ago.

Some people such as fertility expert and midwife Zita West, predict that educated career women will return to having babies in their twenties – and this is a real possibility. A new phenomenon has been identified by American sociologists whereby educated women prefer their husbands to be the main breadwinner and this is now being observed in Britain. Unlike the housewives of the 1950s who had little choice, today's generation of women is building on the advances of the feminist movement to determine their optimum lifestyle. According to research at the University of Virginia, fifty two per cent of modern housewives describe themselves as "very happy" with their marriages, compared with forty one per cent of working women. However, the state of matrimonial harmony is also dependent on other factors such as an attentive and emotionally responsive husband, a sense of fairness in a relationship and a lifelong commitment to the institution of marriage.

Nevertheless, according to the latest figures from the Office of National Statistics a third of women now in their 20s will be singletons by their mid-

40s and of those over half will never have married. It's become more fashionable to be single and increasingly unmarried 'single' partners are acquiring equal legal rights within relationships. The language of the law is also changing: when The Civil Partnership Act came into effect in December 2005, the words 'spinster' and 'bachelor' finally disappeared from the marriage certificate. They're replaced by the unisex title 'single', to take account of gay couples tying the knot under the new legislation.

Unfortunately for them, old-style men are going to be seen as being increasingly inferior and as the war against them intensifies women will increasingly pair up with other women for relationships of convenience. We are likely to see a huge growth in the number of female couples having and/or raising children together. Take Dorothy Berwin and Dominique Levy – Levy an international director of 20th century and contemporary art sales at Christies in New York and Berwin a top film producer originally from London. They fell in love after meeting at a charity film premiere. Berwin has a son from a previous marriage but Levy has had a child since they have been living together – the father is a close friend to both of them. They consciously wanted to have a father who would "*be involved and a really good parent.*" Berwin says her secret for a successful relationship is "*We never get bored with each other... I have met my match.*"

I anticipate we'll see increasing competition between women for the few men who are seen to be appropriate and available. There'll be lots more emphasis on personal branding to win your man and prestige dating agencies will struggle to provide enough men to meet the high quality demanded by the über-woman. There will also be intense competition to buy the sperm of the most eligible men – the best designer babies will be those of tall, athletic, highly intelligent, musical, gifted men donating their most precious and highly sought after seed. As Lori Gottlieb says "*The demographics of women with both the financial means and the temperament to go the sperm bank route alone are so uncannily similar that just as we are all competing for the same kinds of men in the dating world, now we are all competing for the same kinds of genes.*"

Others are just too damned fussy or overly idealistic – in other words just plain unrealistic – as a result of having too much choice. Steve Friedman says "*I want companionship, intellectual excitement, really good sex, fidelity, incandescent, thrilling love, at least one child, the walks under the old oak trees, naturally, someone kind, sweet, not too bossy, not too rigid, not too easily upset by a partner given to occasional bouts of torpor, someone not inclined to express personal hurt with personal attacks. I want a woman who sees marriage as neither the definition of her very essence, nor as a patriarchal plot to enslave and oppress her sisters worldwide. I want a woman whose hopes and dreams I can cheer and support and who will cheer and support mine...I want a woman for whom money is not a big deal, who reads a lot, who's at least a little athletic, who's neater than I am but tends towards bemusement rather than irritation when confronted with towels on the floor.*"

Hardly surprising then that women are increasingly likely to team up with gay men who are generally very house-proud and probably used to picking their own towels up off the floor! Gay man, the 'new best friend' of the überwoman will understand the freedom and the frustration that goes with being childless. He will be equally sensitive and flexible at adopting new trends, provide comfort, understanding, friendship and bring shared common interests to the partnership as they grow closer together. And überwomen will also form partnerships of convenience with gay men to bear and nurture their children.

One thing seems certain; the überwoman is becoming far less likely to produce offspring as 'she' becomes 'he'. Women will increasingly look to choose women for relationships and men will increasingly tend to choose men. As a result the main source of new life on our planet will undoubtedly be the poor and the social underclass. The huge shift in our value structure in recent decades means that we are gambling our future away in many ways. So what else are we destroying in our efforts to live our lives as we please? Read on.

Gambling Our Future Away
"Destructional" Change and the Debt We Owe

George Orwell's *1984* successfully predicted the emergence of a gambling proletariat: "*The lottery with its weekly payout of enormous prizes was the one public event to which the proles paid serious attention. It was probable that there were some millions of proles for whom the lottery was the principal if not the only reason for remaining alive. It was their delight, their folly, their anodyne, their intellectual stimulant.*" Unsurprising then that we should be experiencing such an upsurge in casinos and online gambling!

If you go to Las Vegas you can live the complete disposable dream. In themed 'all you can eat' restaurants you can pretend you are in Paris, Egypt, or ancient Rome whilst being made to feel it is entertaining and 'grown up' to lose your hard-earned money in slot machines or at gaming tables. In parts of America "Racinos" have been introduced - basically race tracks with a casino. What you may not know is that they pump oxygen into the casinos and mix high-energy drinks into your orange juice to keep you awake longer! Apparently such phenomena may be coming to the UK.

Town halls are bidding to open Britain's first Las Vegas style super-casino with up to 1,250 slot machines with unlimited stakes and prizes – no membership is required to access unlimited numbers of tables for poker, blackjack, roulette and other games all available twenty four hours a day. Dozens of casino operators in London are now scrambling for huge drinking and gambling complexes, which will be open till 6 am, sparking 'a reckless gambling explosion.' Prospective developers of 'large' casinos include the Anschutz Entertainment group which proposes a £500 million complex near the former Millennium Dome and MGM Mirage who have proposed a joint venture with Olympia and Earls Court Exhibition centres for an 18,000 square feet venue. Others in the pipeline include a £20 million casino by Caesar's Entertainment at Wembley, a gambling venue as part of the new Kings Cross development, a £9 million casino at the Grosvenor House Hotel and another at the Kensington Roof Gardens. If unsuccessful, they may seek large casino status – with jackpots of only £4000 – conceivably even more addictive than £1 million as it seems more achievable. Even the so-called small casinos will dwarf anything previously seen in Britain with minimum floor sizes of 8,000 square feet and a capacity of around 3,000 drinker/gamblers.

But these days do you need to venture further than your PC or even your mobile phone? Victor Chandler's www.vcpoker.com (using a glamorous IT consultant from Surrey, plus Matt Damon, Ben Affleck, Tobey Maguire and a random 29 year old treasury sales dealer from an international bank based in Jersey as examples of 'regular' players) invites YOU you to 'join the poker revolution'. And what's behind this poker revolution? In short the Internet. "*Where once playing poker meant an inconvenient, intimidating, expensive trip to a casino (if you were lucky enough to live near one in the first place), the advent of online poker rooms has put safe, low stakes and friendly games just a click away no matter what time of day or night.*"

Most of the websites such as www.fulltiltpoker.com use real poker champions to promote the online game. However I was horrified when I recently saw a double-page advertisement in a London based newspaper for www.888.com offering a chance for 'Joe Average' to play in a free online poker tournament.

In their attempt to get people hooked on gambling it seems to me that many of these companies will stop at nothing. Various 'ordinary' people are quoted ranging from a bank manager, a teacher, a student and - the only woman represented - a personal assistant. The banker describes how he is used to handling huge sums of money at work, but gets just as big a thrill from playing online poker *"there is nothing quite like the satisfaction of pulling off a big bluff."* A lawyer claims he has been playing poker since university - *"people might think they are anonymous but you can soon work out what they are up to if you try hard enough"*. A self-confessed competitive and agressive poker player who works in IT says online poker avoids *"the hassle of trying to get all your mates together at the same time."* An advertising copywriter describes how he gets a buzz from *"being creative with his hands."* An engineer says he has learned to pay attention to what other players might have rather than *"falling in love with his own hand."* The teacher finds poker relaxing after dealing with the stresses of the teenage classroom. The student is surprised he isn't out of his league playing in tournaments for money. The personal assistant isn't intimidated or underestimated for being a woman - as well she might be in a casino. An actor adds that he can play poker to suit his unusual working hours and with people from all over the world. The online poker merchants operating in the UK have clearly researched their potential clientele very carefully and some critics might even go so far as to say that they've effectively got carte blanche to bleed their customers dry.

Meanwhile Mr Chandler informs us that *"With the number of online players growing from just 87,000 to over 1.8 million in the space of just two years, the impact of this surge of new blood coming to the game via their modems was best illustrated by the victory of the aptly* (and genuinely!) *named Chris Moneymaker in the 2003 World*

Series of Poker. Having qualified online for about £20, Moneymaker went on to win a staggering $2.5 million in his first ever live tournament." You too can choose to spend your valuable time and any spare cash you have in this way. You can even splash out with your savings should you feel the urge though most people (casino tycoons excepted) have debts rather than savings these days and what you also need to realise is that with online poker - just like online dating - you don't know who or how many people you're playing against!

Just as we will be forced to re-evaluate our lives when our money and our imagination runs out it's predicted from a huge number of sources that we will also be forced to review our future from an environmental perspective. The reality is that we will have to seriously reconsider our means of transportation, the way we heat our houses, the type of products we use and even where we live. When fuel runs out, the geography of the world is going to change. We might like to put our minds to considering the optimum place to live in the world when there is no fuel, rather than worrying about where to place our gaming chips.

Taking a closer look at the environmental issues great minds have been considering for centuries: John Jacob Astor wrote of a capitalist utopia in the year 2000 in his book, *A Journey in Other Worlds*, published in 1894. This was the tale of a company that aimed to tilt the earth in order to create a universal summer - it described how polar bears would have to use artificial ice! Unfortunately Astor's vision for warming up the planet didn't quite materialise as he was killed on the Titanic when the ship struck an iceberg! Ironically, we now know there's global warming which today may inadvertently achieve his ambition. Then, in 1903, William Wallace Cook suggested that in the future there might be an Air Trust, charging for air and a Sun Trust, buying the rights to charge citizens for sunshine.

More recently it has been proposed that there is an increased likelihood of a catastrophic volcanic eruption that could be sufficiently severe to threaten the fabric of civilisation thereby putting events such as the Asian tsunami into the shade. The fallout from such a super-eruption could cause a volcanic winter devastating global agriculture and causing mass starvation. The UK Geological Society has identified at least 31 sites where super-eruptions have occurred in the past including Lake Taupo in New Zealand, Toba in Sumatra, the Phlegrean Fields near Naples and Yellowstone National Park in the USA. There's also speculation that once global warming reaches a certain level, the refraction of light from the sun will itself cause another ice age.

Other sources claim that global warming is a godsend. A hotter planet brings many benefits that humans can adapt well to. Philip Stott, emeritus professor of biogeography at the University of London says "*Cold is nearly always worse for everyday — the economy, agriculture, disease, biodiversity.*" He adds that times of historical prosperity have often been tied to unusually warm periods such as the so called Medieval Warm Period between 1100 and 1300, whereas the Little Ice Age between 1450-1870 was characterised by famines and pandemics. Professor Bjöörn Lombord of the Copenhagen Business School agrees, "*Economic studies clearly show it will be far more expensive to cut greenhouse gases seriously than to pay for the cost of adapting to a warmer planet.*" The predictions for rises in sea level caused by melting of the polar ice caps have also been grossly over-estimated. Claims of five-foot rises have started to give way to less dramatic estimates of between four and eight inches. A recent study found that sea levels around the supposedly threatened Maldives have actually fallen.

Nowadays we tend to spend more time considering life extension techniques than we do considering how to avert ecological disaster. However, such things will all become irrelevant according to those who are seriously concerned

HUBBERT PEAK FORECAST OF FUTURE GLOBAL OIL OUTPUT (CAMPBELL 1996)

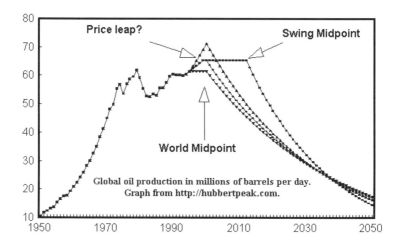

about the dual problems of polluting our planet to destruction and not finding a suitable replacement fuel for oil.

It is variously predicted that global supplies of oil will run out in the next 20-30 years. Without an equally efficient source or sources of energy the world is likely to be a very different place. Some estimate that five billion of the world's six and a half billion population would never have been able to live without fossil fuels and oil powered pumps to drain land or without the chemicals that make intensive farming possible. If oil dries up it has to be assumed that those five billion would starve. Bryan Appleyard, writing in the *Sunday Times* says

"And they won't all be in Africa this time. You too may be fighting off neighbours to pro-tect a shrinking stash of canned food and, when that runs out, foraging for insects in suburban gardens."

In 1956, Shell Oil geologist, Dr M King Hubbert discovered a huge fallacy in the way the American oil industry presented its reports. He noticed that for tax purposes, US oil companies often delayed the declaration of new oil reserves for years, even decades, to give a false impression that new oil was being found all the time. Based on this observation, Hubbert predicted that American oil production would peak in 1969; he was out by one year and pro-duction eventually peaked in 1970 and has declined by 50% since. More recently, petroleum scientists have refined Hubbert's model and applied it to global petroleum reserves. The consensus is that the 'Hubbert Peak' of world-wide oil reserves will occur sometime between 2004 and 2007.

If we look at current figures (see chart below) for outstanding oil reserves, it appears that we have some time remaining before we reach the point of peak oil production. However, according to renowned oil geologist, Dr Colin Campbell, the totals are deceptive because the major oil-exporting nations have major incentives for exaggerating their estimates of reserves so that they can pump more oil. According to the *Wall Street Journal* "*The mystery of Saudi oil capacity bears an eerie resemblance to Saddam Hussein's apparent belief that his scien-tists had developed weapons of mass destruction.*"

The table below is adapted from *Oil & Gas Journal* and US Geological Survey data. The data for these 18 countries represent ninety four per cent of the world's oil reserves and eighty two per cent of its undiscov-ered resources. Dr Colin Campbell calculates that over 300 Gb of reserve claims are spurious (Saudi Arabia, Iraq, Iran, UA Emirates, Kuwait, Venezuela). He also states that much of the undiscovered resources are in fact "unconventional oil" (tar sands, oil shales and other currently unrecoverable resources) and will be much more expensive to extract than "conventional" reserves, and therefore should not be considered as equivalent to reserves. There is the possibility that the US Geological Survey's estimate of world oil reserves is correct and that peak production will not occur until 2020. We might discover a new gigantic oilfield which will further the delay of the peak. But, the essential point is that at

Country	Cumulative Production	Reserves	Undiscovered Resources	Reserves and Resources
Saudi Arabia	71.5	261.2	41.0	302.2
Russia	92.6	100.0	68.0	168.0
Iraq	22.8	100.0	45.0	145.0
Iran	42.9	93.0	22.0	115.0
UAE	15.1	98.2	7.0	105.2
Kuwait	27.6	97.5	3.0	100.5
Venezuela	47.3	83.3	17.0	100.3
USA	165.8	50.7	49.0	99.7
Mexico	20.5	50.4	37.0	87.4
China	18.8	24.0	48.0	72.0
Kazakhstan	3.2	17.3	26.0	43.3
Canada	16.1	5.1	33.0	38.1
Libya	19.0	22.8	8.0	30.8
Nigeria	15.5	17.9	9.0	26.9
Norway	6.3	11.3	13.0	24.3
Indonesia	15.2	5.8	10.0	15.8
UK	12.3	4.6	11.0	15.6
Algeria	9.1	9.2	2.0	11.2
TOTALS	**621.6**	**1052.3**	**449.0**	**1501.3**

LEADING OIL COUNTRIES PRODUCTION, RESERVES AND RESOURCES (BILLIONS OF BARRELS)

some stage in the fairly near future we are going to run out of oil. More worryingly there are no completely cogent plans in place to deal with this eventuality when it happens.

As the world's oil reserves dwindle, oil will be harder and more expensive to extract and energy prices will skyrocket as we compete with China and India for increasingly limited supplies. America has encouraged and invested in an automobile-centred suburban way of life to the exclusion of all alternatives. And as in the case of the response to post-hurricane Katrina New Orleans, there seem to be no contingency plans! Nevertheless the sprawling, con-sumerist, capitalist lifestyle that industrialised nations have come to take for granted is likely to come to an abrupt halt at some stage in the not too distant future.

This doomsday scenario has been variously predicted by authors such as James Howard Kunstler who, in *The Long Emergency*, predicts a new Dark Age. Regardless of what ener-gy source we believe might replace oil, we have to build the structures – nuclear plants, hydrogen fuel stations, solar panels the size of New Mexico, massive forests of windmills and so on from an oil platform to begin with. Big cities and their suburbs will collapse, along with industry and mechanised agriculture; serfdom and horse-drawn carts will make a comeback; there may well be a depopulation of the American Southwest (impo-tent governments may even engineer designer viruses to cull the surplus population) and Asian pirates will plunder California. We will experience wars not just over oil but also over fresh water which is not only becoming scarcer but which also requires massive amounts of energy for desalination. Americans will eventually have to live in smaller towns and eat locally produced food. One of Kunstler's main conclusions is that human populations will shrink until they reach equilibrium with the natural resources on the planet.

James Lovelock in his book *The Revenge of Gaia: Why the Earth is Fighting Back and How We Can Still Save Humanity* believes that climate change caused by pollution from fossil fuels is not a matter of man destroying the planet but of man bringing about the downfall of man. His theory is that the earth unconsciously regulates itself much like our own bodies, in order to maintain conditions conducive to life. He implores us to stop using fossil fuels now and revert to nuclear fission as a means of energy until such time as we have the technology to use safe and renewable nuclear fusion.

My view is that perversely, running out of oil may eventually result in ecological salvation for our planet. Initially we will almost certainly see more global competition for oil – potentially leading to wars, as well as more "globalisation" of oil fields by consuming nations: - one only has to look at what is happening in Iraq today. But we also need to consider man's ability to adjust to a more modest lifestyle that is more in harmony with the planet's resources. With the help of the Internet and modern communications we are all undergoing a rapid re-education programme. Over the next few years there is likely to be a drastic re-evaluation of the world's problems and a major re-targeting of our resources. Most of us are already all too aware of the fact that resources are limited – we are now beginning to appreciate the fragile balance of our planet and the fact that we need to save some resources for future generations. This means we are also likely to be living, working and holidaying more locally than at present.

In the UK reviving our coalmines and making them a primary source of fuel for generating electricity could be the most cost effective way of meeting our medium term fuel needs. A new technique for burning coal that releases a minimum of carbon dioxide has been developed and Britain has enough reserves of coal to last up to 100 years. Existing coal-fired power stations may also be upgraded to minimise carbon emissions by the introduction of more efficient boilers.

We are already focusing on solving energy and transportation issues with environmentally friendly cars such as the G-Wiz (www.goingreen.co.uk). Many of us are driving the Toyota Prius or even opting to travel by bicycle. Already firms such as Climate Change Capital (www.climatechangecapital.com) which runs the Carbon Disclosure Project listing the FTSE 500 companies' annual carbon emissions is beginning to gain more prominence in the City. The era of 'intelligent fuel' is already upon us with the development of the 'Env Bike' (www.intelligent-energy.com) - a hydrogen and oxygen powered motorcycle. Elsewhere a hydrogen-fuelled aeroplane is currently being tested. Eventually we will strive to limit travel and we'll learn to cherish the real benefits and advantages of local community life.

We are also beginning to realise how supermarkets are destroying the culture of our local communities at the same time as we become generally more health conscious. So small specialist farm producers, growers, regional suppliers and local shops will become more significant. The film, *Walmart: The High Cost of Low Price* challenges the threat posed by out of town 'supercenters' to smaller independent retailers in the USA. As well as minimising the 'food miles' travelled before produce reaches our plates, we are now asking for a greater choice of groceries and foodstuffs, as opposed to the limited range and mediocre quality, white-labelled products piled high in sprawling retail parks. UK retail sales were approximately £260 billion in 2005 according to the

Office of National Statistics. Online sales made up 3.1% of this figure compared with 0.1% in 1997. - sales at Tesco accounted for £719 million of Internet shopping. However consumers are increasingly demanding organic, seasonal and local produce as awareness of the benefits to health and the environment has become more widespread. Each year £120 million is spent at farmer's markets and this amount is likely to become more significant over time. Supermarkets are also being forced by public demand to stock more local produce or lose out to increasing numbers of local delicatessens and small specialist shops offering a more natural and unique range of produce. The market for seasonal produce and farmers' markets will increase. Hopefully we will suffer less from obesity and chronic illness caused by too much consumption of fast foods and too little physical activity. We'll also start wearing more Fairtrade and environmentally-friendly clothing such as Romp's organic designer sheepskins and Stella McCartney's vegetarian shoes.

In China, British engineering firm Arup is building an eco-city called Dongtan. The first phase is due for completion in 2020 providing homes for 80,000 people powered by renewable energy, self-sufficient in water and with all foods sourced from surrounding farmland. The scheme is being built on China's third largest island, Chongming and is intended eventually to have half a million inhabitants. Petrol and diesel cars will be banned and household waste will be removed via underground tunnels. Taking the lead from China, The London Development Agency is working on a mini eco-city in Newham – with plans for 1,000 homes to be built on the express understanding that they do not add to global warming.

We've been living with a false sense of security for too long. It's going to be a huge effort to stop our environmentally destructive practices but at least we've become aware of the extent of the problem before it's too late. For most of us our aim is to live happily and healthily together. And nowadays, we also expect long and happy lives - just look at the growing industry in life extension techniques and ever more ingenious efforts to maintain a youthful appearance.

The Quest for Eternal Youth and Beauty

Breaking Biological Barriers to Change

We also have a problem in recognising the difference between appearance and reality. So called 'Reality' TV has become a replacement for the old-style 'freak show' and *schadenfreude* (taking pleasure in other people's misfortune) is a big new trend in television viewing. A typical programme of the type is called *Bingers* about the secret life of a bulimic mother. Such programmes are occasionally given a tenuous credibility by supposed experts who are brought in to offer help and reform to ordinary people and their lives. In fact they often make their subjects look and behave like the talentless and frequently irresponsible celebrities that they spend millions of pounds a year buying magazines about.

In fact such programmes are usually a poor excuse to laugh at the deficiencies, failings and misfortunes of others. *Make Me Perfect*, a new TV makeover series by the producers of *Big Brother* was recently looking for 15 female recruits with a poor self-image to "*undergo the total physical, emotional and mental transformation of a lifetime!*" So presumably they were looking for physical, emotional and mental wrecks to salvage? In fact ongoing emotional and mental change is perfectly normal during one's lifetime as are the physical changes associated with natural human ageing.

Unfortunately this emphasis upon the physical above every other aspect of our being is becoming all pervasive. New cosmetic treaments are constantly being developed to replace older versions that fall unacceptably short of our new standards. The race is already on to find a way of using stem cells as a means of skin rejuvenation. So don't just think about buying some new clothes, why not get a new face and a new body? Plastic surgery isn't yet so commonplace as to have outgrown its appeal and this despite the fact that we live at a time when yoga and spiritual awareness are also hugely popular. What will follow plastic surgery in our affections - maybe gene therapy and cloning? Posh, Becks, Brad, Kate, Siena and Angelina might one day be appearing in more places than you'd otherwise expect.

One plastic surgeon recently commented that an extraordinary number of clients ask to look like David Beckham *"But when the request comes from a 50-year-old man with a double chin, it's hard to sound very encouraging. Some people seem to think I'm a magician, not just a surgeon."* A recent *Sunday Telegraph* Magazine article entitled *The Line of Beauty* mentioned a lady who had four litres of "yellow gloopy fat" removed from her thighs. Afterwards, she commented that she felt lighter, but that *"I'm not sure anyone looking at me would notice a real difference. And it's not like I've been transformed into a confident person. I suppose I didn't expect to be, but when you go in for something like this you have to check yourself, because you start thinking anything's possible."* Another story was about a 22 year old law student who had silicone implants in her calves (the first woman in Britain to do so) because she felt they were too thin. She was also given an accentuated cleavage. She subsequently lamented the effect surgery had on her love life, complaining *"men just treat me as a sex object."* When a 61-year old grandmother from West London had a neck and face lift, she looked like a victim from *Crimewatch* after the operation. Did she feel younger? *"Not exactly,"* she replied, *"I still feel mortal, but I know that if I drop dead tomorrow, at least I'll look good in my coffin."*

There's a huge trend today towards improving our looks. From *blepharoplasty* to *mastopexy*, from *thermosudation* to *erbium yag* laser treatment – one company called the Aesthetics Corporation carries out over 500,000 procedures a year in areas like these, with long latin-dervied names probably to make them sound more complicated and expensive than they really are. Ironically, one of the latest behavioural addictions is a compulsive attachment to cosmetic surgery!

Or you could opt for a nutria-genetic diet - eating food matched to your individual genetic make-up based on a sample taken from a cheek swab to lower the risk of the diseases to which you are most prone. As far as medical advances are concerned scientists hope that stem cells can one day be used to re-build tissue and grow new organs. This will significantly increase life expectancy since drugs currently can do little more than slow the onslaught of degenerative diseases. Researchers at an American company, CyThera, have already developed a technique that is "*a critical step in generating scientifically and therapeutically useful cells.*"

Meanwhile David Cohen, writing in the *Evening Standard,* tells how a Harley Street plastic surgeon has launched plans to sell a controversial anti-ageing drug. The use of this drug in the United States is based on a 1990 study published in the New England Journal of Medicine by Wisconsin researcher Daniel Rudman who compared two test groups of elderly men taking injectable HGH (human growth hormone) producing changes equivalent to reversing ten to twenty years of ageing. HGH was originally developed to promote growth in those with dwarfism. The drug has numerous potential side effects including hypertension, tumours and diabetes. In fact those using the drug who have an undetected cancer are likely to cause the cancer cells to multiply more quickly ensuring a more rapid demise. Moreover studies on animals have shown that rodents with lower levels of HGH actually tend to live longer. Harley Street surgeon, Jeya Prakash was nonetheless inspired by the work of Julio Garcia whose Las Vegas clinic, Ageless Forever, has been selling HGH for some years (at $600 for a month's supply). Prakash insists that "*taken in small doses, research shows that human growth hormone is as safe as vitamin C.*" He adds that the drug is taken by most doctors in America who are fully aware of the risks involved. Both he and his wife have taken the drug for a couple of years and attribute their youthful looks at the ages of 55 and 48 respectively to its positive effects. Prakash believes that HGH is set to follow the course led by Botox - another product that started out unlicensed though became officially approved for cosmetic use in 2005 - and will become a huge business.

As we strive for cosmetic perfection, anti-abortionists and ethical groups are up in arms about the increasing number of terminations that are carried out for treatable birth defects. Figures from the National Office of Statistics show that between 1996 and 2004, twenty babies were aborted because they had clubfoot. This is one of the most common birth defects in the UK affecting between six and seven hundred babies a year and can usually be corrected without surgery – using splints, plaster casts and boots. Statistics also show that four babies have been aborted since 1996 because they had webbed fingers or extra digits all of which can also be corrected by simple surgery. In 2004 it emerged that a baby was aborted at twenty eight weeks after scans showed it had a cleft palate. A curate called Joanna Jepson lost her case to bring criminal charges against the doctors involved and condemned such actions as *"fostering a disposable attitude to human life."* Julia Millington of the Alive and Kicking campaign commented, *"It seems we can no longer tolerate any imperfection. Babies are at the mercy of ultrasound scans and what they may disclose."*

For years, scientists have been predicting that once we have mapped all human genes a new era of personalised medicine will follow and we will start to see people living well into their early hundreds. Designer babies with 'disease-resistant genes' are already being born – A British woman has recently become pregnant using a controversial IVF technique that weeds out embryos that might develop cancer in later life.

In the United States prospective parents have been using a procedure known as preimplantation genetic diagnosis, or PGD, for more than a decade to screen for childhood diseases that are potentially untreatable. England has now approved the use of PGD for breast and colon cancer risk. This has led to critics posing moral questions such as who decides what is a serious enough potential condition to warrant testing. They also fear that PGD for cancer could be the first step towards a genetic class divide with the wealthy becoming more genetically pure than the poor.

Adult stem cell research is already happening. People with appalling burns can be saved by their skin stem cells while stem cell skin grafts are already being used to treat leg ulcers and stimulate the leg to remember to heal itself. With cancer it is often the stem cells that cause the damage by multiplying out of control. Skin cancer is conventionally treated with drugs and radiotherapy but these can damage the good stem cells, as well as the bad. Professor Watt at the University of Cambridge Institute for Stem Cell Biology is trying to find ways of reminding stem cells that they should be producing normal cells rather than mutating. Cures for Parkinson's disease, cancer or diabetes are some way off but there is no doubt that they are already 'work in progress'. The University of California has done research that would allow us to re-engineer eyes using retinal implants and a human bladder has been grown from tissue cells at Wake Forest University in Northern Carolina. Stem cells can be used to renew the heart, injectable muscle implants are being used to impel movement in paralysed muscles by electrical stimulation and electrodes implanted in the brain can help patients control the tremors associated with Parkinson's Disease. Malcolm Gladwell, author of *The Tipping Point* concurs, "*We now go to lengths that would have seemed unthinkable just a century ago to save and extend life.*"

The flip side of using techniques to extend life is the creation of an ageing population. This is a problem of unforeseen dimensions. The population in the so-called developed world is simply ageing too fast. In Britain, for instance there are now around 16 million people aged between 40 and 59, a figure projected to rise by 15% over the next 20 years. If born today you can expect to live 25 to 35 years longer than your Victorian forebears, up to 45 years longer than your medieval ancestors and at least 55 years longer than your Stone Age precursors. Life expectancy at birth increased by almost a decade in the first 50 years of the NHS. Figures from the UK Office of National Statistics show that between 1970 and 2004 life expectancy at age 65 in England and Wales increased by four and a half years for men and three and a half years for women. By 2004, men aged 65 could expect to live to the age of 82 while women on average could expect to live to the age of 85. Evidence suggests that levels of ill-health and disability in older people at any given age are falling. The gerontologist, John Grimley Evans, has said that we are spending "*a longer time living and a shorter time dying*".

In fact another possible war of the future could be between the old and the young, as they fight for increasingly limited resources in times of ever-greater change. The young may well become unwilling to support the ageing population or to pay taxes for pensions they themselves may never receive.

Simon Jenkins writing in the *Sunday Times* says, "*The bias against age is a fetish that infects everything from politics to marketing to culture. It bears no relationship to intelligence, spending power or balance of population. Active voters over 50 dominate the polls, they watch more television, buy more books, form the majority of church-goers and visitors to galleries, museums, country houses and gardens. By 2020 a quarter of Britons will be over 65.*" He claims that young people are mostly poor, busy and self-obsessed and that it's the old who have the money, time, outside interests and strength in numbers to dominate the public realm. "*Collectively they constitute what passes for community in Britain.*" The 18-30s have been classified as Generation Y and face a crisis caused by loans to finance higher education combined with the pressures of a hugely inflated housing market and a looming pensions crisis. The over 50s now own four fifths of the nations wealth and pensioners alone have assets of £500 billion. There has been a shift of wealth in favour of the older generation. The older generation (dubbed Generation X) can afford to try to keep themselves looking and feeling young but Generation Y is growing up fast by having to work round the clock to make ends meet, to get onto the housing ladder and to pay off existing debts.

There well may be a time when some parts of the world will be centres for elderly populations and others for younger ones. We may even have old and young countries. Britain, France and Northern Europe/Scandinavia may well be older (with the exception of some cities such as London and Berlin attracting the young from other countries) whereas Southern Europe, Africa, West, Central and South America would be younger (with the exception of certain locations that have become centres for retirement). Places of rapid development such as India and China would also be young whereas anywhere where the rate of change is slowing down such as the East Coast/Mid-West USA or Canada would generally be older.

The combination of differing birth rates, the geographical movement of people around the world and the break down of traditional family structures creates a population much more easily defined by age. In turn this affects the nature of future economic and social development. The elderly will be compelled to establish localised networks for mutual support rather than depending on younger members of the community for assistance during their old age. But an ageing population of pensioners also implies the need for a degree of support from young people which may lead us to question the UK government's fifty per cent target for young people in higher education and suggest instead that there should now be a focus upon skills that the economy needs. Many graduates now simply opt for what appear to be safe jobs offering a good pension. Others opt to take any job that is available to pay off their debts.

It is due to the fact that people are living much longer these days that we are so unfamiliar with the concept of death. We are used to the idea of living to the age of 80 and beyond. We expect to live a reasonably long and active life. Yet we assume that more old people having a longer old age equals more people in expensive misery. It seems that we no longer have any respect for the elderly because they are expensive to keep, their ugliness disgusts us and we feel that they don't contribute to society. Yet in fact what we have is a much larger and a much healthier older population and when *we* are old, we will want nothing more than to enjoy our extra years to the full. According to the *Sunday Times,* Debbie Harry, the 60-year old singer delights in the fact that *"Guys still hit on me. I still get a little bit of action! God, I hope that it doesn't stop for a while."* The likelihood of humans living beyond the age of a hundred is currently limited mainly to those either living in those parts of the world with the most healthy lifestyle and diet or to those with sufficient funds and access to the foremost medical/alternative technology. But in every case it still doesn't matter how rich and famous you are, whether or not you exercise regularly or abuse your body by drinking or taking drugs. Ultimately, the truth is that as human beings, each and every one of us is mortal … and accidents, as well as medical conditions, do happen.

So maybe it's the popular opinion that the old and diseased are useless that has exacerbated the recent media fascination with assisted dying? Many cite the absence of high quality palliative care contributing to the suffering of terminally ill patients becoming so unbearable that such patients would simply prefer not to exist. The term 'assisted dying' refers to the practice in which a physician prescribes the medication that a patient can take to end their own life as opposed to 'voluntary euthanasia' where the physician would actually help the patient to die. Lord Joffe recently tried to pass a bill through the UK's House of Commons to enable doctors to prescribe drugs to terminally ill patients in severe pain that would end the patient's own lives. Peers backed an amendment to delay the bill by six months but there is increasing pressure from lobby groups and charities such as *Dignity in Dying* as well as from the general public to give people the right to decide when they die. The main concern from opponents is that it is but a short step from assisted dying to euthanasia. Lady Finlay, a professor in palliative care said, "*Let us get on with working for patients to live as well as possible until a naturally dignified death, not get taken up with becoming complicit with suicide.*" The slippery slope towards suicide has even sparked a furore in the Netherlands, the first country in the world to allow baby euthanasia.

Of course it's different when a baby or a child is terminally ill. If you visit www.childhospice.org.uk you will see that '*highly trained staff will be able to help your child and the rest of the family - in a purpose built hospice, or in your own home - with the medical and emotional challenges that having a life-limiting condition can bring over many months and years. Children's hospices provide specialist respite care: regular short stays for the child or for the whole family together. They also provide emergency and end of life care; specialist advice and expertise; practical help and information and 24 hour telephone support. Above all, they are positive places, helping children and families to make the most of life. Children's hospices are committed to working with families from all faiths, cultures and ethnic backgrounds and they fully respect the importance of religious customs and cultural needs that are essential to the daily lives of each family.*' One of the nurses from Christopher's Hospice, Bridget Turner, explained to the *Sunday Times* Magazine that the original meaning of hospice was a place to rest on your journey. "*We don't have the power to change the end of the story, but we can make a difference along the way*", she adds. These children can't be made better but they can be made happier. They will even be helped to understand what will happen to them reading books such as *Goodbye Mousie* and *When Dinosaurs die*.

Yet it seems there is rarely such preparation for adult death. Aren't we just fooling ourselves that serious illness or death are never going affect us? Death has been a taboo subject for far too long. We are shocked when people die slow and painful deaths from cancer even though most of us know someone who has been affected by the disease. We read books like those written by cancer victims such as John Diamond and survivors, such as Brandon Bays yet if we hear that someone died in hospital it's almost as if we can't understand that this is possible. We don't seem to be able to accept death as the fact of life that it is. In the developed world we are so used to such low rates of infant mortality that when we hear "*My baby died!*" we recoil with horror and sorrow - but sometimes this happens. Death is the reality of life: but I predict that its history is about to change.

The Future of Death

Changing the History of Mortality

Death is becoming a major issue. Only now are people realising that the one certainty in life is not only a significant landmark to work towards but that death is also a huge moneymaking enterprise! Indeed the UK Chancellor is trying to cash in on this by imposing a super tax from April 2006 on lump sum pension payouts that are in part intended to cover funeral expenses.

56 year-old New Yorker, James Atlas, recently authored an amusing book about growing old called *My Life in the Middle Ages*. He describes how the passing of friends turns his address book into a 'necropolis' and claims that "*Getting into a cemetery is going to be about as competitive as getting into a private school.*" Atlas's book, an entertaining and poignant memoir of middle-aged, middle-class anxiety has become something of a generational talking point in the USA. This concept of writing memoirs, of letting others know the story of your life your ambitions, hopes and fears is not such a new trend. However, recently it has been given renewed impetus and added importance through the growth of the Internet. Weblogs have become a primary means of expressing opinions in every possible subject area.

In Britain there are now more than 400,000 online diarists – nicknamed "bloggers." Globally there are 14 million blogs, with a new one every second. So writing diaries has become fashionable again – see www.blogger.com, www.myspace.com and www.diaryland.com. A recent study of the phenomenon of online diary writing found that people writing them felt happier and more organised. With increasing pressures caused by juggling work and home life the process of expressing inner-thoughts in a non-judgemental environment can be highly rewarding and have positive psychological and emotional benefits. Blogs have become a way of feeling wanted and getting more out of life. They are also an expression of the 'me culture' where everyone feels the need to be heard and be a celebrity in their own right. There's even a new agency called www.scoopt.com, linking bloggers directly to the press. Orville Gilbert Brim, a psychologist completing a book called *The Fame Motive* claims that the desire to network, write a screenplay, a memoir, or appear in a reality TV show is related to the realisation that even if we don't achieve fame in this lifetime there may be a chance of it posthumously. Quoted in the *New York Times* Dr Brim says "*It's like the belief in the afterlife in mediaeval communities where people couldn't wait to die and go on to a better life…*" So does this account for the growing popularity of suicide bombing among terrorists?

There has always been a fascination with the concept of everlasting life and now there are even blogs for the afterlife: A company called "Afterlife Telegrams," a supposedly non-profit making organisation proposes for those who wish to contact a dead relative or friend to make a 'donation' of $5 per word. The message (which can be posted on their website) is then memorised by a terminally ill volunteer who endeavours to pass it on when he or she dies. The fee, depending on the wishes of the messenger, is then given to a relative, a charity, or put towards the payment of medical bills. All the volunteers have a prognosis of survival for a year or less. The service has been condemned as predatory and cruel by religious and charity groups – but the company's founder is adamant that the telegrams help people though he adds "*Of course, we cannot guarantee that the message will be delivered successfully, but we do ensure that the messengers have promised to do what can be done to deliver their telegrams.*" The founder also admits not only that the possibility of reincarnation could make the successful delivery of a telegram impossible but also that there can't be any guarantee that the messenger will end up in the same spiritual realm (ie heaven, purgatory or hell) as the deceased.

There is also talk of bringing the dead back to life. Apparently scientists in America have made this a very real possibility by reviving dogs after three hours of clinical death. The Safar Centre for Resuscitation Research in Pittsburgh has perfected a 'suspended animation' technique in which the veins are emptied of blood and filled with ice-cold salt solution. The dogs' breathing, heartbeat and brain activity stopped and they were scientifically dead. However, after several hours the blood is replaced and revived by an electric shock and the dogs can be brought back to life. Tests carried out afterwards have shown that they are perfectly normal with no brain damage. It is hoped that this 'suspended animation' technique will soon be developed for use on humans who are victims of penetrating trauma, such as gunshot or stab wounds, causing cardiac arrest.

Some of us believe in re-incarnation – certainly many who have survived near-death experiences. Is there anything in this? Or is it just that to be human is to suspect that there is a higher reality and that the world is not as obvious and banal as it appears to be? If we except those who are genuinely religious and who therefore have foundations and structures of worship and the afterlife already in place there is also a wealth of alternative options available to the rest of us. You can even create your own model. In addition to conventional religion there are countless cults, crazes and alternative therapies. In the words of

Bryan Appleyard *"These exotic spiritualities attract popularity because they are different enough to be fashionable and because, compared to the rigours of religious observances, they are cost-free."*

Even science and particularly physics, conventionally regarded as the enemy of religion and spirituality, has seized upon the fashion for mysticism and seems increasingly to be favouring the spiritual. Appleyard cynically says *"You don't actually have to do much to feel all dreamy and significant about quantum theory or cognitive science – and the Beatles seemed to do little more than chill when they hung out with the Maharishi."* I anticipate that scientific endeavours will increasingly call upon 'other than earthly' explanations. Dr Rupert Sheldrake (www.sheldrake.org), a biologist, has recently been given £100,000 to investigate whether we have a sixth sense. This study which will involve research carried out mainly using tests conducted via the Internet is being backed by a trust set up to research the paranormal, administered by Trinity College Cambridge.

Mix and match belief systems have been the focus of much recent publicity, such as that accorded to the BBC television programme, *Heaven and Earth*. However in this age in which we all seek to be globally interlinked we need to envisage a broader way in which people of all religious persuasions and ethnic backgrounds can potentially be joined together – united in their common humanity. Living TV already generates revenue of £28 million per year from spiritual programmes alone... So, think BIG, think the Internet and digital media!

Could the Internet be the key to everlasting life? Is the Internet the future of death itself? Yes plastic surgery can keep you looking young; gene therapy may even keep you alive longer but my prediction is that the Internet and the size of the computer server that your information is stored on may actually be what keeps your name alive for posterity.

A Radio 4 programme about a Help the Aged report on the Church's role in the handling of death expressed how inadequate it seemed to be. In a world with such an ageing population where death is all around us, isn't it strange that we so rarely ever talk about the process of death or the spiritual questions it raises? This seems to be the case even in church. Death is somehow denied and swept under the carpet and all manner of inventive synonyms are used to disguise this eventuality. We 'pass over', 'pass away', 'become deceased'… but rarely are the words 'die' and 'dead' used (even by funeral directors), except in clinical circumstances, perhaps at mortuaries.

The realm of death and the dying has become too much of a taboo area. Very few people would know what to do if somebody suddenly died nor probably would they have much idea about how to organise a funeral, even though such a thing is more likely to be required of them than having to organise a wedding! According to the National Hospice Foundation one quarter of American adults over forty five say they would be unwilling to talk to their parents about their parents' death – even if they had been told they had less than six months to live. Half of all Americans said they were counting on friends and family members to carry out their wishes about how they wanted to die – but 75% of them had never spelled out those wishes to anyone. The president of the National Hospice and Palliative Organisation said *"Americans are more likely to talk to their children about safe sex and drugs than to their terminally ill parents about choices in care as they near life's final stages."*

A feature in the *New York Times* Magazine entitled *The Struggle to Create the Good Death* focuses on our ambivalence about dying, our belief that it is something over which we have some control and how our *"death defying culture has led to a system of care for the terminally ill that allows us to indulge in the fantasy that dying is somehow optional."* It is strange that death often comes as something of a surprise since people who die tend to be sick and old already! The field of palliative medicine (the word 'palliative' being derived from the Latin 'to cloak' or 'to shield') has become big business. Where the hospice has become the place of last resort for the dying, palliative care offers pre-hospice prevention and relief of suffering for the terminally ill. With so much knowledge and understanding about medical conditions and life expectancy it is extraordinary that even a top palliative care expert says, *"You can study around it, but with death, like black holes, there's something intrinsic to the very process that defies our ability to analyse it."* The moment of death is considered too sacred and intimate for scientists to study even though many people die with tubes and wires protruding from them. Scientists have investigated the altered states of consciousness of the dying but many still consider it as belonging to the realm of the spiritual, rather than the scientific.

But our views on death are about to change. At a time when things are out of date before they have come into being, when we are all asked to think in terms of 'leaps beyond,' I have noticed that surprisingly people are looking to the past more and more for their inspiration rather than to the future. History is becoming big business and the reputation of historians is growing as we look to them for a sense of clarity, purpose and direction about where we have come from as well as where we are going and why. As Alvin Toffler says *"Whatever happened to some men in the past affects virtually all men today."*

Genealogy websites such as www.ancestry.co.uk which helps us trace our ancestors, memorial websites and forums for sharing life experiences such as digital time capsule, www.diaryofmankind.com are also becoming increasingly popular. In October 2006 *The National Trust* organised a project called One Day in History. Contributors, including the staff and pupils at 29,000 schools, were asked to write between one hundred and a thousand words about their day as a 'blog for the national record.' Despite all the 'next big things' that are advertised and bandied about around us it's the little things that make us happy – reminiscing over an old family photograph, finding an old coin in the back yard, or a jug in the attic, watching the dog chase its tail and soaking up the children's laughter as they play.

The Victorians' obsession with death will return. Ornate headstones, ornaments and all sorts of vintage paraphernalia will appear alongside graves, in crematoria and remembrance parks (see www.memorialsbyartists.co.uk). People are already beginning to visit old cemeteries in greater numbers and some, such as Highgate and Kensal Green in London offer regular guided tours for visitors. An exhibition was recently held in the Dissenters Chapel in Kensal Green cemetery of photographs taken in and around the area. The actress Sharon Stone has recently written a 'reflective text' to a book called *Something to Hold*, which features black and white photographs of gravestone angels. Grayson Perry's August 2006 art exhibition *The Charms of Lincolnshire* featured a Victorian Hearse and a cast-iron child's coffin accompanied by ceramics, embroidery and dolls – satirising cosy village Britain which "*was a candlelit, backbreaking sexist tubercular child-death hell.*"

Old scents and smells that remind us of our forebears will gain renewed popularity. Sepia photographs, domed displays of wax flowers, ornamental urns and treasure boxes of our memories will reappear to take us back to a 'better time' – a time of strong family values, of common bonds, unity and stability. The value of shared memories will be appreciated as never before.

Trend forecasters (www.trendwatching.com) have coined the term 'life-caching' to describe the trend of collecting, storing and displaying one's entire life for private use, to be perused by friends, family or even the entire world. They claim that a new range of technologies and tools including memory sticks and high definition camera phones is leading to "*an almost biblical flood of 'personal content' being collected... to allow for ongoing trips down memory lane.*" Nokia's 'lifeblog' software for instance lets users automatically arrange all messages, images, notes, videos and sound clips they capture with their mobile phones into a PC based diary. Key cord memory sticks are the new Asian fashion accessory and are worn around the neck so that consumers can show, play and share their entire life with whomever, wherever! Life caching is likely to make sharing an experience as valuable, if not more valuable, than the actual experience itself.

I foresee a time when the dead and the living will be shown equal precedence. And why not for even in the midst of life we are in death? The growing inter-est in digitising old films and archived information, in researching genealogy, using 'in memoriam' websites, of leaving something permanent behind (if not, or in addition to having children and providing future generations) will all be focused on the Internet.

We will also start to see online cemeteries. In fact in the future the combination of lack of space for burial plots and our increasing intolerance of germs spread by diseased bodies may lead some governments to require all bodies be burned. Online cemeteries may become one of the few places where our lives can be commemorated. Above all our overwhelming desire to be remembered for posterity will be satisfied by our ability to post our autobiography on a website or for our life story to be viewed via digital media - to be experienced, admired and learned from by others. Beyond money, sex and mortality, we will be remembered for our contribution to future generations via the Internet.

PART TWO

DEATH TRENDS

Handling the Dead
The Historical Legacy in Britain

Ways of removing the dead from the living have changed little during the course of human history, with burial and cremation being the two main forms of funeral. This chapter is a factual outline of the historical background to the treatment of the dead in Britain. It is worth noting the relative influences of functionality, design and public sector intervention, in order to appreciate the inspiring new approaches of recent years.

Until the mid-seventeenth century high-status burials took place inside churches in vaults sunk into the floor but the majority were interred in parish churchyards. This monopoly was first challenged in the 1650s when Nonconforminst burial grounds like Bunhill Fields on the northern fringe of the City of London began to be opened. The earliest Jewish burial ground, in London's East End dates from 1657.

Throughout the seventeenth and eighteenth centuries there was increasing criticism of burials in Church of England graveyards and vaults in urban areas. The comparatively small number of gravestones in a churchyard can belie the number of bodies buried there. The churchyard of St Martin-in-the-Fields was only 200 feet (60 metres) square yet in the early 1840s was estimated to contain the remains of between sixty and seventy thousand persons. Churchyards were full to overflowing which created unsanitary conditions and spread disease. From the mid-seventeenth century onwards people like Sir Christopher Wren, John Evelyn and Sir John Vanbrugh revived the Ancient Roman idea of burial with cemeteries on the outskirts of town. The first such burial ground was opened in Bloomsbury in 1714.

As the idea of the neoclassical cemetery gained ground, outdoor burial became increasingly attractive. In the 1770's urban cemeteries were created in Edinburgh (Calton Hill) and Belfast (Clifton) but not until 1819 was the first public cemetery in England opened, in Norwich (The Rosary). During the 1820s, several more provincial cemeteries were opened but there was still no national movement for cemetery creation. There was no legislation to allow public authorities to set up publicly accessible cemeteries. Instead, most were created by private Joint Stock Companies set up expressly to make a profit from the interment of the dead. Private enterprise was responsible for the first public cemetery in the capital: All Souls' Cemetery at Kensal Green which was opened in 1833.

By 1850, urban churchyards had had their day. Over-full, exclusively Anglican and suspected of being sinks of contamination they were closed in large numbers over the next few years. A public alternative to the profit-making private cemeteries was needed: The Metropolitan Interment Act of 1850 allowed for the provision of publicly funded cemeteries in London - and was extended across the country by an Act of 1853.

This ushered in a boom in the construction of public cemeteries by publicly financed Burial Boards run by parish vestries (the ancestors of today's local authorities). Scores of cemeteries were set up in the 1850s and 1860s. In many cases the architect who designed the mortuary chapels and other structures was also commissioned to provide the layout but other sites were laid out by nationally known landscape designers. Many of these landscapes were of very high quality incorporating careful compositions of chapels, lodges and catacombs – and enhanced by memorial structures and planting. By 1900 there were few towns that didn't have their own public cemetery. Not only were these repositories for the dead but they were also places of resort for mourners and others – and, as cities expanded, so surviving areas of green space assumed even more importance.

Meanwhile there were medical and scientific concerns about urban cemeteries that had now become dangerously full due to the dramatic growth of many cities during the Industrial Revolution. In some cases rotting corpses were buried too near the surface and could often be smelt in church crypts. There was pressure for sanitary reform which – combined with progress in town planning – led to the legalisation of cremation.

In 1874, the Cremation Society was founded but the first official cremation did not take place until 1885 at the great cemetery of Brookwood, outside Woking. (So special was this cemetery which remains the largest in Europe, that it even had its own railway line to bring entire funeral corteges from Waterloo Station almost to the graveside). In the 1890's Manchester, Glasgow and Liverpool built crematoria but it was not until 1902 that the greatest of all such installations the Golders Green Crematorium was opened in north London. Further crematoria set in their own distinctive landscapes followed throughout the twentieth century as the cremation movement accelerated.

By the Edwardian period however, the "Great Age of Death" had passed its zenith. Burial and mourning customs were changing, moving away from the elaborate Victorian ritual of commemoration towards a more private, less showy grief. The mass deaths of two world wars and the resulting need to bury large numbers of men who had died away from home made cremation seem an increasingly acceptable practice. At the same time the dignified restraint of the cemeteries and memorials of the Imperial War Graves Commission provided a model for a new style of remembrance. After World War II most cemeteries were laid out on standard grid patterns. Lawn cemeteries were introduced with memorial stones set flat into the grass, providing a large expanse of open lawn and making for much easier maintenance.

Churchyard memorials were not really seen in large numbers before the 17th century when the bereaved were allowed to put up almost anything ranging from huge vaults and obelisks on the one hand to stone angels, skulls and figures on gravestones. But between the two world wars regulations were introduced restricting what was permitted in churchyards. Everything had to be easy to maintain and the most decorative monuments permitted were borders of polished granite infilled with grass. Nowadays each of forty three different dioceses has its own regulations. As monuments and memorials have to be approved by the local vicar, artistic originality is limited.

There are approximately 7000 hectares of cemeteries in England – district, town and parish councils and London boroughs owning the majority of them. In fact, the exact number of cemeteries is not known, but a reasonable estimate might be between five and ten thousand. A typical cemetery is ten acres in extent, and was opened between 1850 and 1880.

Based on data collected in 2000 on 1416 cemeteries eighty percent are still open (defined as having twenty or more new graves available for burial) and a further eleven percent were limited (with fewer than twenty new graves available). Up to sixty percent of burials today are "re-opens", ie. burials in existing graves where space is available. In fact 75 percent of cemeteries that were established in the period from 1851-1914 are still open.

Although only twenty eight per cent of all burials are whole body burials, there is growing evidence that Britain is facing a shortage of burial space. This is in part because of our unwillingness to re-use cemeteries as is the norm in most Continental countries. A detailed burial survey has not been completed for London but anecdotal evidence suggests that the problem is not restricted to large metropolitan areas. Elsewhere burial authorities, some in rural locations, also report having problems in financing the purchase of new land for burial and/or being able to secure appropriate land at a reasonable distance from the community they serve.

Donald Boddy, the remembrance park designer, explains that typically in England and Wales people do not "buy" graves; they buy the right to be buried in a particular place in a cemetery. In fact graves can often accommodate up to four coffins on top of each other known as a private or "purchased" grave. The owner of the burial right retains the right to decide who is buried in a given plot but the duration of these rights is defined by the burial authorities themselves.

When cemeteries were first established burial was in perpetuity. Nowadays perpetuity is defined as 100 years. Most burial authorities sell rights that last perhaps 50 years. Some people are buried in public graves whereby they buy interment but do not have the right to decide who else may be buried in the same grave. Both private and public graves are subject to legislation on disturbance of human remains. Once interred human remains cannot be disturbed without a special licence from the Home Office. The Times reports that the cost of a simple burial service has increased by more than sixty percent in recent years to an average of £3,307.

There are 600,000 deaths a year in Britain but most human remains end up not in the ground but as ashes. The cost of cremation has seen similar rises to an average of £1,954 over the past five years. Smoke from crematoria containing plastic and metal products compounds the greenhouse effect. In fact sixteen per cent of Britain's daily mercury emissions come from cremation alone and the formaldehyde in embalming fluid has contaminated watercourses.

Today, the fastest growing environmental business in Britain is the disposal of the dead. Cardboard coffins, DIY funerals and woodland burial sites are taking an increasing proportion of the undertaker's business. There are now more than 120 sites where headstones are not permitted and most burials are in cardboard coffins so leaving no mark on the environment. A tree is planted on each grave, creating woods in the countryside that are kept in trust for the enjoyment of future generations.

As Douglas J Davis says in his book *A Brief History of Death*, "*Contemporary life, especially for those in successful parts of developed societies, has become increasingly grounded in personal choice over lifestyle, accentuated and facilitated by consumerism. Within such market-economies it is possible to speak not only of lifestyle, but also of death-style.*" This is explored more fully overleaf.

A Fresh Approach to Death

The Ecological Perspective

The word 'cemetery' is generally associated with sadness and loss. As remembrance park designer and owner Donald Boddy says, "*Many of us have walked through a cemetery and not felt anything other than a sense of function conveyed by rows and rows of headstones. A similar image in a war cemetery where rows of identical headstones may stretch into the distance may create within us a very different emotional reaction – a feeling of great sorrow at such a waste of lost lives and loves.*"

Partly as a reaction to the impersonality and anonymity of traditional cemeteries and in response to the growing trend for environmentally friendly or alternative lifestyles we are now seeing a fresh approach to the treatment of death from a number of quarters. As with most new trends anyone involved in each of these projects is totally passionate and devoted to the work they are doing.

One such is Roslyn Cassidy owner of personalised funerals company, Green Endings (www.greenendings.co.uk): who had been inspired by Barbara Butler's small Somerset company to "*do funerals differently.*" As Roslyn says, "*Traditional funerals do a good job, but they feel empty.*" So she set up an alternative to the traditional funeral business where funerals could be "*celebrations of life.*" The fact that most deaths occur hidden in hospital and are then taken over by funeral directors has led to a feeling that "*death has been taken out of our hands.*" Roslyn saw a gap in the market and decided to offer a choice of how and where funerals are conducted. "*People's lives are so individual it just seemed crazy to me that a funeral is like a conveyor belt, when it is possible to create something completely different.*"

Operating mainly in London and within the M25 most of Green Endings' funerals are conducted either at Golders Green, Islington or St Pancras cemetery and crematorium. These may sound very unglamorous locations especially if as one of Green Endings' clients expressed it, you have a *"dread of men in black coats, of hardwood coffins, brass handles, pompous hearses and all the traditional paraphernalia of death."* However Roslyn describes her ceremonies as *"gorgeous."* Coffins are painted or draped in beautiful fabrics and services often include poetry readings, music, singing, dancing and photographic exhibitions of the dead. Instead of formal floral displays each person brings one flower to lay on the coffin. Cassidy believes that funerals should be unique and celebrate the life of the deceased.

Personalising a funeral could involve anything from a religious, humanist, or traditional ceremony to a graveside picnic or a woodland burial. A variety of coffins is available and all are made from natural materials including plaited bamboo and papier-mâché recycled newspapers. Woodland burials require biodegradable coffins and the grave either has a tree planted by it or is surrounded by freshly planted bulbs or wild flowers. The Natural Death Centre founded the Association of Nature Reserve Burial Grounds in 1994 and sites include the South Downs Natural Burial Site in Hampshire. Green burials place death within the *"richness and fecundity of life and so reclaim it from the medical profession."*

As far as the coffins are concerned Cassidy explains that the bamboo comes by ship, rather than by air and is packed *"like Russian dolls, with 5-6 in a pack, so the space is well-used."* She adds that the bamboo comes from sustained forests in China where the workers are paid relatively well. Willow and wicker coffins are made in the UK and Poland but they are half the price when sourced from Eastern Europe. Green Endings offers a range of prices so people can choose to pay more and buy British if they prefer. Unvarnished pine coffins are also available – they are shipped flat-packed from South Africa as there is nothing like that available from the UK. Traditional wooden coffins (from sustainable sources) are also an option – it's really up to the customer as the service is personalised to their requirements. The company also offers some green alternatives for funeral transport – a motorbike with a sidecar is very popular with older people who had a sidecar after the war. This uses less fuel than a hearse but more than a horse-drawn funeral carriage.

Around seventy per cent of funerals conducted by Green Endings involve cremation, which coincidentally is the industry average though it is no greener than burial. Cassidy believes that freeze drying (of which more later) will become the thing of the future. "*It's a shame we can't put bodies out in a bin bag with the rubbish, on the compost heap, or donate them to science, but the great majority of bodies need to be properly disposed of*," she says. Nevertheless, only around five per cent of bodies need to be embalmed due to the excellent refrigeration available nowadays. She always gets a specialist in to do this where necessary and ensures that a non-formaldehyde embalming fluid is used.

One of the most challenging aspects of Roslyn's work apart from its 24-hour nature is the physical handling of bodies. People don't appreciate how heavy bodies are – including even the most petite and frail of old ladies! The material used for coffins needs to be strong: bamboo for instance is so strong that it is used for scaffolding in Asia whereas the use of cardboard is limited to those whose bodies are not overweight.

Interestingly, another company, Dutch EveryBody Coffins (see www.every-bodycoffins.com) has started to produce modular, self-assembly coffins that come flat-packed (Ikea-style) – the pieces simply click together. These eco-friendly coffins are a low cost alternative to expensive caskets and are aimed at offering a dignified solution for burial and cremation in disaster areas and epidemic situations. The website shows the specification of the coffins, which come in adult and child sizes, are light-weight and easily transportable in large quantities – The load bearing capacity is not, however, mentioned!

Roslyn describes how this is the most life-affirming job she has ever done and explains how gratifying and emotionally rich it is to work with people who are bereaved, to put the funeral together and to provide a meaningful "send off." She also explains how her work has made her appreciate the fragility of life, "*the seconds between life and death are immense.*" Above all, it makes her appreciate her own life and think about safety issues – driving, crossing the road. Life can so easily be snuffed out and there are so many complex ways in which people can die.

Roslyn's personal philosophy is interesting. She would like to be remembered as someone who lived every minute of her life fully. She believes that "*human beings are everything – the connections, closeness, relationships, history between people – nothing else matters, or comes close.*" She also appreciates working with and co-operating with people on projects, collaborating closely with others to achieve something that excites her.

As it turns out, Roslyn was raised in a Catholic, Irish, Afrikaans family with six children and says she is culturally a Catholic. She doesn't believe in reincarnation, but as a scientist she says she doesn't know what happens to the heat and electricity in the body – the energy, or transfer of electrons – at the time of death. She would herself like to have a woodland burial in a bamboo coffin with all her friends and family crying, laughing and telling stories about her whilst enjoying great food and music. She thinks it's important to play hard and to cry hard but also to sort things out with people to apologise for places where you messed up and to let people know that they matter to you.

Roslyn sees her role as preparing for the funeral, getting the body there and directing the proceedings. She is also effectively *"raising the consciousness about the ordinariness of death, not hiding it."* She says some people use the process of planning for the event as a vehicle for grieving and can become totally obsessive about details and organisation whereas others are totally hands-off. *"It's interesting to see how people cope. One of the most fascinating aspects is working with different 'cultures'."* Roslyn isn't referring to ethnicity here but to the culture of each family. *"The dynamics of each family is different – who's top dog, who does all the work surreptitiously, or unobtrusively behind the scenes. You get to see that your family is as functional or dysfunctional as all the others – but they are all just doing the best they can."*

Roslyn loves making the event work for as many people as possible – especially since there are often warring factions! A funeral is a social event that brings people together in a way that may not happen again. *"Lots of healing can be done at a funeral when people who haven't spoken for years end up in the same room."* Roslyn particularly enjoys the healing aspect of her work – she feels that whoever is co-ordinating the event, whether it be her, or one of her assistants, often ends up being very close to the family – loving them, cheering them on, encouraging them not to be scared and to be ready to leave someone dear to them – this is such an achievement for her. She loves the people side of the business and considers herself especially fortunate since the funeral director is often the only person present who is a stranger. *"People are so vulnerable at this time: I see the real person - I would never get to know people like that otherwise."*

Another proponent of the personalised approach to dying is the aptly named Donald Boddy - a rather eccentric and award-winning designer and owner of remembrance parks (www.ecopartnerships.com) who has a uniquely philosophical approach to life and death. Donald is currently completing work on his latest venture, the Mayfields Remembrance Park at Eastham in the Wirral Peninsula overlooking the River Mersey. When making a speech about the new site, Donald explains, *"Life is full of uncertainty and subject to constant change. In this climate only two things are certain: the undeniable fact of our birth and the inescapable conclusion of our death. The space in between is an empty page, which must be filled to give it meaning and substance. Love is the meaning, a subject of huge mystery, but one we grasp instinctively until the object of our affection is taken away. We mourn and grieve for others, whereas in reality we mourn and grieve at the terror of their departure, leaving us alone and exposed."* To Donald, cemeteries are more than just a place to bury a loved one – they are places to remember our loved ones, to reflect on life, past events and loved ones: places to find emotional healing, comfort and hope for the future. This is why Donald calls his cemeteries remembrance parks as he feels cemeteries are for the dead whereas parks are for the living.

Indeed he considers cemeteries to be far removed from the traditional cultural beliefs of life and death as viewed by history and explains that current moves within both the industry and individuals have reemphasised cultural ideas and the importance of remembrance. There is clearly a revival in the cultural interpretations of death and a new stress on the importance of an environment of remembrance both of which are in marked contrast to the traditional cemetery with its lack of personal associations. In the past fifteen years Donald has seen the creation of over 180 alternative and private burial sites – on average one per month. One of his concerns is to ensure these new facilities provide a long-term sense of place beyond a simple fashionable environmental concern and that they meet the short-term and long-term needs of the bereaved and their families. He believes that the Victorians had a vision when they created many of the old cemeteries which has sadly been lost in recent times especially following the loss of the personal cemetery keeper and gardener to whom people could talk and learn about the gardens. He has his own cemetery rating system which he calls the 'Three T's' and advises anyone choosing a cemetery to use this evaluation. The first 'T' is for 'talk' - he feels you should be able to find someone to talk to or ask a question. The second 'T' is for 'tea' because talking is a thirsty business and the third 'T' is for 'toilet.'

Donald says *"all that we do should have a purpose, a story and a meaning."* His aim is to create a sense of place that may be associated with happiness as well as sadness and that can provide for emotional healing rather than depression. At one of the parks he designed, the West Pennine Remembrance Park (www.remembranceparks.com) overlooking the moors midway between Bolton and Blackburn, they have been holding regular events for five years including concerts where visiting families can have a picnic close to the graves of their loved ones whilst listening to the music of remembrance. There is a park pavilion and event area that also serves as a bandstand. They have a four-seater buggy to provide easy access to all burial areas and children, especially, enjoy a wild ride down a steep embankment! There are logs close to graves to sit on, a meeting room with refreshment and toilet facilities.

The newest site in the Wirral village of Eastham where twenty acres of grassland is being transformed into six themed gardens and island sanctuaries is designed with the help of Feng Shui experts and TV gardener Chris Beardshaw (www.mayfieldspark.com). Four of the gardens are for burial and the fifth will contain a series of small gardens for meditation and healing. The sixth garden is a children's nature garden. The park is designed to meet people's needs in terms of the plot layouts as well as responding to religious and cultural requirements. There is an olive garden with a vineyard as well as herb and rose gardens. An earth spirit garden celebrates harmony with nature and the natural earth energies. There is also a celebration garden of culture, faith, music and art with an amphitheatre - and a garden of personal islands of remembrance set in a sea of wild tall grasses. Many of the islands are linked by bridges, symbolic of the link between life and death – the Latin word for priest *Pontifex* means a bridge builder – someone who could bridge the link between heaven and earth. Donald sees the park as providing an opportunity to build bridges between people, faiths and cultures and is creating a trail for all ages to help people explore the many different cultural and religious views of life and death. He is also creating story-telling areas and a secret garden for children to play in. He believes the park can provide understanding, trust and harmony between people, faiths, cultures and their own relationship with nature.

Donald claims that the problem with traditional cemeteries is that they contain only sad memories. He encourages people to plan ahead, to create a final resting place that the family is familiar with. They can visit the park; attend musical events, talks and workshops. *"It's about coming to terms with life and death and laying down happy memories in a place we are familiar with… Creating a sense of belonging so that we feel relaxed, at peace and at home so that when there is only one person visiting there is a reservoir of happy memories to draw on."* He explains that they are changing the concept of funerals, which are currently about transportation between many points to a rigid timetable, *"Mayfields Park is not like anything you have seen before. Within each garden there are celebration areas in which funeral services can take place, enabling families to gather and stay in one location to have a celebration event and ceremonial march to the burial location, followed by a traditional wake – all planned to meet their personal requirements".* He wonders why people don't plan a funeral as they would plan a wedding and make it a memorable event.

According to Donald you simply have to find the burial area, plot size and garden that suits you and your loved one. *"People can also choose according to the view, whether it's of the river or the woods…It's not about taking the next available plot, it's more like buying a house!"* Buyers can choose either a small plaque if they have no one to bury but still want a loved one to be remembered – or they can purchase their own garden: prices range from £350 to £100,000.

Each plot has a path and access to electricity and water together with space for a seat. Donald also offers security in the form of twenty-four hour guards, fences and swipe cards to gain access – so not just anyone can wander around. Not quite the sort of security that's needed in some developing countries (of which more later) but certainly enough to make your Mum feel safe sitting overlooking the estuary by herself. Donald says "*if you don't feel secure, you can't relax.*" His own measure is that his park should be "*safe enough for a blind man to fall to sleep.*"

Donald is a true visionary. He envisages that one day his remembrance parks will offer a place that holds the whole family history. He is creating facilities at the park for families to record their history which will be accessible on the internet (www.diaryofmankind.com) and on handsets at the graveside. For this reason his family burial plots are sold with thousand years burial rights - unlike most cemeteries that are usually only available for any part of a hundred years, and could be reused or turned into a car park thereafter. As Donald says "*somebody never dies until they are forgotten - immortality is achieved through remembrance.*"

At Easter he held a ceremony to "*awaken the spirit of the site.*" A willow fence of memories was created by making and adding personalised willow additions – a willow leaf for £2.50, or a willow snail for £5.00 with a small engraved copper nameplate. As well as an African drumming band, a folk quartet and a Celtic harp and flute duet, there was a Liverpool street band to march out the route and summon the spirits of the site. The names of all those remembered at the site are chanted - as they will be for a thousand years to come – although once the site gets fuller, each name will only be chanted at one of four annual ceremonies – perhaps according to that person's favourite season or when their birthday happened to fall. From the initial chanting, Donald hopes "*to find the rhythm of the site*" and to create a piece of music that becomes a signature tune for the remembrance park.

Donald is creating his own above ground burial tomb and is going to invite his artist friends from around the world to help him decorate and furnish it. He intends to spend eternity relaxing on a sun-lounger in pleasant surroundings! He is also going to advertise internationally for applicants for the position of the park's spiritual guardians who will be buried in special vertical chambers partly above ground and located in strategic positions. One of Donald's other plans is to install a seventy-five foot tall timber tree sundial he purchased from a garden festival. He says you'll be able to see it from the other side of the estuary and it will become a new local landmark.

There are future plans for an End of Life Centre within the park grounds. This is where you will be able to come and stay with your family to die. Alternative health care and therapies will be available here and there will also be a park newsletter called the Tranquil Times. Donald has thought of everything!

Despite Donald Boddy's creative line of work his own views on death are as remarkably down to earth as is his commercial common sense. He wonders why when we are all born to die we spend so much time and effort trying to prolong our lives – he doesn't see the point of working towards having the corpse that's in the best condition in the graveyard! He says *"we are so concerned with the welfare of animals yet when they no longer have any quality of life we have no problem in deciding to have them put down......so why do we adopt a different set of principles for human beings – it seems that life has to be preserved at all costs, regardless of pain and suffering. Why not allow people to have a choice and to come to terms with the end of life and move on? If we are physically incapable of looking after ourselves, or our purpose for living has been removed, why not let us die?"* The Natural Death Centre handbook (www.naturaldeath.org.uk) has a chapter on the politics of dying and advises people on the preparation of a Living Will to define how, or for how long they are to be treated in the event of being incapacitated.

Donald doesn't see death as a taboo subject. To him taboo has more to do with black magic. And, as for religion, he sees that as an excuse for blaming someone else – it's simply the opportunity for guidance based on a third party point of view – *"God defines the point of death, which is simply opting out of the issue."* In any case, he claims, *"most people just go with the flow. They're too busy bringing up their families and working to pay for their living to put their life into context – they tend not to think about how they'd like to be remembered or what they'd like to leave behind as a legacy... And then it's too late, they end up with their funeral being held in a sterile and unwelcoming environment with a service conducted by a vicar who didn't know they existed until they died and finally being laid to rest in a location alien to their lifestyle and one which may put their family at risk when visiting."*

He ponders on the potential implications of a world pandemic affecting large numbers of the population. He comments that we'll be okay for healthcare arrangements but no one has thought about burying the dead. He predicts that mass graves will have to be dug leading to public outrage, because as things currently stand there is insufficient public burial space and people have not planned ahead for such events by at least ensuring their family has its own burial location.

Donald's sanguine approach to the ecological dimension of his work is also measured by a healthy dose of reality. Whilst the running and management of his newest site will be as eco-friendly as possible - he has signed up to the Clean Merseyside Centre's 'Buy Recycled Code' and is committed to using recycled materials but it's really up to the individuals purchasing the plots as to what they decide to do with their land and how they wish to be remembered. There are basic planting and design guidelines for each garden, but if they wish to have a designer terracotta pot from Italy on their plot, then that's fine – in fact Donald will be selling them.

Like Roslyn Cassidy, Donald Boddy agrees that freeze-drying is the way forward. Susanne Wiigh-Masak, a marine biologist from Gothenburg in Sweden has developed an eco-friendly form of corpse disposal by freeze-drying called 'promession'. The burial of corpses generally known as earth or casket burial has been the most common way of laying the deceased to rest since the 12th century. The regulations for burial that were created at that time have not changed appreciably in the last 900 years! Our knowledge has increased considerably over this time however, and we have much more information about the health and environmental problems caused by burial as well as an understanding of oxygen and its role in the process of decomposition.

There is no oxygen at the depth caskets are currently buried. Oxygen is required to convert corpses to mulch otherwise they simply undergo a long and slow rotting process caused by the bacteria that live on sulphur. The final remains leach into the soil and follow the ground water, affecting and in some cases ruining our drinking water … until sooner or later they reach the sea where they worsen eutrophication (the process whereby a body of water receives nutrients that stimulate excessive plant growth).

The increase in cremation was a response to the rapid rate of urbanisation of the 19th century and at the time was an innovative solution to serious sanitation problems. However, from a biological point of view, cremation is neither ecologically correct, nor environmentally sound. Each cremation takes about twenty litres of fuel and half a kilogram of activated carbon for cleaning the flue gases. Despite this, a large quantity of flue gases, also containing mercury from fillings and toxic plastic products from hip and other joint replacements are released into the air. The Swedish National Environmental Protection Agency estimates that one third of all the total mercury emissions in Sweden come from the country's 73 crematoria. The resulting ash that is buried in the soil or spread over the earth gets flushed into waterways by rainwater and also ends up in the sea affecting eutrophication and causing oxygen depletion.

Wiigh-Masak wanted to "*combine biological knowledge with a dignified and ethically correct way of being remembered by ones next of kin.*" Her aim was to preserve a body in organic form allowing for a shallow burial in living soil that quickly converts to mulch. For this, her company, Promessa, has developed the following process: firstly within a week and a half of death the corpse is frozen to minus 18 degrees centigrade and submerged in liquid nitrogen. The corpse is then very brittle and, using vibrations, the remains are reduced to an organic powder which removes the water that makes up 70% of a normal-sized body. The now dry powder is passed through a metal separator where any surgical spare parts and mercury are removed. The organic powder is hygienic and odourless – it doesn't decompose when dry and so can be kept for as long as required until the funeral. The ideal coffin is made of a biodegradable substance such as cornstarch which can be buried in a shallow grave a few inches underground unlike conventional burials that are six feet deep. The living soil turns the coffin and its contents into compost within around six to twelve months. Relatives may then plant a tree or a shrub on top of the grave to absorb the nutrients from the remains and complete the ecological cycle making death the provider of new life.

The town of Jonkoping in Sweden is turning its crematorium into a "promatorium" later this year because of the multi-million pound cost of introducing mercury filters to meet emission targets. Swedish national burial law is currently being updated to accommodate this practice which is expected to spread across the country over the next few years. International interest is considerable. In the UK there have been concerns that the procedure would breach English cremation laws though legal experts and church leaders in Scotland recently said they had no objection to the new method of disposing of the dead. Emeritus Professor Kenyon Mason talking to *The Scotsman* said " *So long as you don't interfere with public health and safety, there are very few rules and there is nothing to stop you burying your aunt at the bottom of your garden if you wish.*" Tight guidelines on cremation have been introduced because the body is completely destroyed, which could have implications in crime cases. Professor Mason said *Promession* created similar legal concerns, but would not be covered under cremation legislation so "*I don't see why it shouldn't happen, so long as it is not offending against public health or local government regulations. Sooner or later we're going to have to stop burying people because all the space will be taken up.*" A spokesman for the Church of Scotland said "*There do not appear to be any theological implications with this method of disposal, but it sounds like an appropriate thing from an environmental viewpoint.*"

The use of cryogenic technology not only reduces the impact on the air we breathe, since there are no emissions of mercury or smoke, but the green-house effect is also reduced by using liquid nitrogen instead of combustibles. The use of embalming fluid is completely eliminated. The fact that the contents of the grave are reduced to mulch within a year means that the remains do not impose any impact on the environment. This could make it possible to place gravesites anywhere – on family property, or other places with emotional ties to the deceased, or next of kin. *The Scotsman* points out that burial is not the only answer to ecologically sound body disposal: The Parsees of Mumbai in India leave their dead on top of Towers of Silence to be eaten by vultures while in the Solomon Islands the deceased are laid out on a reef for the sharks to eat. According to Maori custom the dying are placed in huts which are later burned. The corpse is then dressed for public viewing. After a few years, the bones are cleaned, covered in red earth and placed in a special cave.

Meanwhile in Newcastle, a charity called the Anglo-Asian Friendship Society is campaigning for Hindus and Sikhs to cremate their dead on funeral pyres at open-air ceremonies. Davendar Ghai, the charity's president, said that open-air cremations were essential to the process of reincarnation. "*Reincarnation is a foundation of the faith and the older generation fully believe that, without these essential last rites, the soul languishes in restless torment.*" He claims that many Hindus and Sikhs are offended at having no alternative but to use the gas-powered furnaces of a conventional crematorium. Many relatives choose to take the remains to India to avoid risking the "catastrophic consequences for the departed soul" of a failure to observe all the rituals of the funeral pyre. Newcastle council is seeking advice and says that outdoor cremations are illegal due to the pollution they cause, let alone the smell of burning human flesh. The Anglo-Asian Friendship Society claims that whilst cremations in crematoria are regulated there is nothing stating that an outdoor funeral pyre is illegal and that they will comply with all planning and environmental requirements. The charity has already identified sites for pyres across the country and will take its case to the European Court of Human Rights if it fails to win backing. And it appears that they intend to carry out their wishes to set up a site near Newcastle shortly even if they are breaking the law.

On a more material note James Langton writing in *The Telegraph* reports that some of America's richest men are defying the old adage that you can't take it with you and are planning to enjoy their fortunes from beyond the grave. They are preparing not only to have their bodies deep-frozen at the moment of death but also to use a tax loophole to bequeath their wealth to themselves. Believers in cryonics sign up to private companies which for $150,000 will suspend their remains in liquid nitrogen and store them for hundreds of years to come. So far 142 people have been placed in cryonic suspension at the Alcor "*life extension facility*" in Scottsdale, Arizona. Some have taken the cheaper option of "neuropreservation" whereby only the head is preserved. They will also invest millions of dollars in "*personal revival trusts*" until future medical technology makes it possible to bring them back to life and they will be able to fund their living expenses in, say, 23rd century America. Don Laughlin, 75, a casino owner from Nevada, has decided to leave his preserved remains $5 million so he has "*a better chance of coming back.*"

Back in the real world I interviewed a sample of ordinary people who have suffered bereavement to find out more about their personal experiences – their opinions towards the way funerals were conducted and their feelings about death. All names have been changed.

Bereavement and Immortality

Experiences from the UK

Until the past couple of decades, no one dared to mention sex. Now it's death that's kept under wraps. Sex pops up everywhere. It's almost impossible to avoid in advertisements, on TV and the Internet. Strangely we worry about the quality of death for animals such as turkeys, but rarely do we ever consider our own end. How will we die, by whom and for how long will we be remembered?

Talking to ordinary people who have suffered bereavement we suddenly become aware that everyone goes through similar feelings and emotions at this sad time. Yet we do very little to prepare ourselves for the experience of losing a loved one. Death is something that happens to other people and is always devastating when it happens to someone dear to you.

As Douglas J Davis in *A Brief History of Death* says "*The death of others is one of the prime moments in life when individuals are prone to a sense of loss of purpose and of the worthlessness of life: why carry on when those who make life worth while have gone? It is precisely at the time of bereavement that less-stricken members of society bring their sense of hope to bear upon the hopeless. It is through funeral ritual that a people tell their stories of the meaning of life and enact their rituals of transcendence.*"

It is, of course, possible to speak about many things as a "loss" – divorce, redundancy, the loss of a limb, of youth, of a pet perhaps? But nothing compares to the loss of a partner or relative. And it's made worse by the fact that a funeral is rarely talked about until the person you need to talk to about it has died.

Joan Didion in her book, *The Year of Magical Thinking*, explains how on identifying the body of her husband of 40 years *"I was so determined to avoid an inappropriate response (tears, anger, helpless laughter), that I shut down all response."* She thinks part of the problem is that there's pressure in 'civilised society' to play down the need to grieve, almost a conspiracy to treat mourning as a morbid self-indulgence. Craig Brown, reviewing her book adds that it's as if *"Death now occurs off-stage, well away from the land of the living, and society reserves its admiration for those who hide their vulnerability and get on with life."* I decided to interview some ordinary people living in the UK to find out if the 'stiff upper lip' approach to bereavement prevailed:

Richard is 33 years old and was one of four boys in a family of 5 siblings. He was 5 years old when his sister died, 6 years old when his father died and 18 years old when one of his brothers died. Richard has no significant memories of his sister's death from cancer. His father also died of cancer a year later and his brother who suffered from Downs Syndrome survived operations on four holes in his heart before eventually contracting septicaemia following an operation that led to his death.

Richard recalls how as a child he visited his father in hospital. He remembers how high the hospital bed was and that his father's hair was falling out. As he was sick for quite a while Richard doesn't have any memories of his father being healthy. He didn't attend the funeral and says his mother tried to shield him as much as she could. He was looked after by lots of people to the extent that he had no clear identity of where he lived. He just noticed that people were "ginger" around him and was aware that something wasn't right. At the time of his father's death Richard's family were living abroad. There were lots of changes. He had to learn English for example. He didn't really experience any feelings of sadness at the time because he was young and was protected. His father was only 26 or 27 when he died and his mother has since remarried. His stepfather is wonderful but his personality is very different from his real father's. He is curious to know what it would have been like growing up with his real father and whether or not they would have had more interests in common.

Richard's coping mechanism has been to become very resourceful and self-sufficient as a result of his experiences of bereavement. Like most teenagers, he did go off the rails but this was probably exacerbated because of what happened. His brother's death was completely different. Richard was at school when he was informed that his brother who was then at Harefield Hospital had died. His parents were at the hospital with him and Richard was being looked after. When he saw the school secretary walking towards his classroom he instinctively knew what had happened. He cried once and only then. He swallowed it and kept it inside. He wasn't able to express his emotions at the bereavement. Even now he likes to take control in dramas but the cost is high in terms of personal injury. Because he didn't want to deal with his emotions he became manically depressed shortly afterwards and tried to commit suicide. Richard claims he simply dealt with and got over this episode in his life because he didn't want to burden his family. He has taught himself to forget his feelings – so much so, that he now has a very bad short-term memory. Richard says he feels guilty that he has trained himself to forget and deliberately put things out of his mind but that this is what has kept him sane.

He lived abroad for a number of years and when his grandmother died he wasn't able to attend her funeral. He now regrets this, saying "*a funeral is a rite of passage that brings us close to someone's life. It is a full stop that makes everything more real. It's why all civilisations around the world do have some sort of burial ceremony.*" Richard says he has been conditioned to accept cemeteries for what they are: beautiful places, well manicured with ornate headstones – "*they fit into the whole grieving process, they are obviously morbid places, but it seems the right place to be.*" His brother was buried with his grandfather and then his uncle was buried "a few graves up." He adds, "*You do need a sense of occasion and a funeral ceremony is a special event, albeit a tragic one.*" To Richard, dealing with death is a very personal issue, "*A problem is as big as you make it – if you commit suicide because your dog dies, it could be equal to your whole family dying – it's a question of degrees and of personal experience.*" Richard's view is that you have to give as much emotional support as possible at this difficult time. Death is such a difficult subject to broach that there's no right or wrong way to do it, "*the people left behind are the ones to take care of.*"

So, how would Richard like to be remembered? "*I'd like to have a cartoon character named after me … and be remembered for being a kind and honest person with real moral values.*" He'd like to be remembered by his son – but would also hope to be remembered forever. Richard has been successful; he's had a family and has now simplified his life. Having worked for an American company and jetted all over the world, "*just vanity*", he is now trying to live a more organic life. Richard's both religious and a scientist – a practising Jehovah's Witness, who would donate his organs! He believes there is a god but not necessarily a single being – "*the Bible is just a means of God communicating in a way that we can understand.*" To Richard it's how you deal with the way that God has communicated that's important. "*Love boils down to love of your neighbour and love of God.*"

In business, for example, there's a tendency to be commercial and to extract the maximum for the shareholders. If you are mindful of other people's needs, the planet becomes sustainable, values improve and society becomes successful rather than being destroyed by declining morals." To Richard, the most important type of love is that of self-sacrifice – putting others before yourself, firstly your family and then everyone else. *"It would be nice if people could remember me for that."*

Richard says he is now also rather cynical about death – he almost expects things to go wrong. He's not sure how he'd cope if his son now aged one and a half were to die – but he almost expects something to go tragically wrong. However, he's lucky that he's got the hope of resurrection and doesn't know how people without any faith can cope. With faith he is okay – just.

Luke is neither religious nor spiritual. To him, "motorcycling is a spiritual experience, a feeling of freedom." When Luke imagines death, he doesn't think the soul goes anywhere. "Death is like a sleep without dreams." Now 30, Luke lost a very close friend and flat-mate at the end of November 2004. His friend was German and had gone back to see friends in Germany for a party. He got quite drunk and was prone to sleep walking. Some time between three and four o'clock in the morning he fell from a third floor balcony. It was thought that he had woken up and felt sick, so went to the balcony. He spent two weeks in hospital in a drug-induced coma before he died at the age of 34.

His friend's brother telephoned Luke to tell him that he had been in an accident and was in hospital. The seriousness of his situation didn't sink in. When his friend's death was reported, Luke says he felt minor shock and cried for about 30 seconds. He then wondered what to do with his friend's "stuff" – as he had been living in his flat before his death. He decided to hire a van with two other friends to take the belongings over to Germany at the same time as attending the funeral. Unfortunately they got stuck in the most appalling traffic jam on the way to the ferry and missed the boat they were supposed to take. They arrived late and missed the funeral but went to the graveside to pay their last respects and attended the wake at his friend's parents' house.

Luke had never been to a funeral before and was amazed at how tall the mound of earth and flowers was. One of his friends sprinkled marijuana over the top of the grave. He had imagined funerals to be solemn affairs, but Luke was surprised by the celebration of his friend's life that took place, which he put down to the family being very Christian. His friend was "very loyal and lived his life in a philosophical and principled way without preaching it." At the time, his friend was working for Luke doing filming. Luke enabled him to do things and go to places that he wouldn't have otherwise experienced. In fact, Luke would like to be remembered for creating opportunities for he and others with limited resources, for creating something great out of nothing. At his own funeral, Luke would like "a wake where people could have a really good drink and really enjoy themselves." He remembers his friend from time to time and he would expect others to remember him "forever."

Luke says he feels indifferent to death. He "was neutral" when his grandmother and grandfather died – and also when his friend died. He wonders if he is supposed to feel more than this. Luke confides that he had mixed emotions at the time of his friend's death. On one hand he was quite sad, but on the other, he felt a certain excitement about having everyone rallying around him. He actually enjoyed the buzz of organising their trip to Germany for the funeral and of being the centre of his friends' attention. He even enjoyed being the first to tell his friends about the tragic accident. Luke says he feels guilty about this.

One thing about bereavement is that everyone reacts to it in their own unique way. It can be problematic if individuals are told there are stages of grief that they should experience, which in fact they do not. However, it can be far worse if the process of grieving is denied.

Hilary experienced this when her first child died 20 weeks into her pregnancy. Now 48, Hilary was 33 when she went into early labour and her baby was delivered stillborn. She was stunned. She had experienced no difficulty during her pregnancy. She had done her research and thought that at around 15-16 weeks, the shifting of the life-support machine to the placenta was the last major hurdle in the gestation process. She was then "set" and had lowered all of her barriers and self-protection mechanisms. Her baby (a boy) was due in the first week of December and she had been planning Christmas with her new baby.

There was an investigation and no cause of death was found. It was just something that happened. For Hilary the most devastating thing was that because her son was less than 28 weeks old, he was not able to have a funeral. The baby was the property of the hospital to be disposed of as waste in an incinerator. Hilary explains, "*Miscarriage is a particular form of bereavement that everyone wants to hide – it is preferable to pretend that it didn't exist.*" The best the hospital could do was to offer the services of a priest who, due to the age of the foetus, was not allowed to carry out a baptism. Hilary and her husband had not been able to look at the baby, but the priest took the cover off and they saw he was perfectly formed with all his fingers and toes. The priest prayed for and gave the baby a name. They called him Alistair.

Hilary had previously been very outgoing, but became very internal. On leaving hospital - where no counselling was available - she shut herself off from the world at large. After a week away from her job she returned to throw herself into her work and shut down outwardly. The only structure to her day was when she was at work. For months afterwards if she saw people who were pregnant or pushing prams she felt she had to run and hide. She couldn't bear to talk to people. Her stomach turned to knots if she heard someone was pregnant as she thought *"please don't let it happen to them."* She started to hear babies crying in the house, in the bottom of cupboards and drawers. A common feeling after miscarriage, though not often talked about, is the feeling that you have literally 'lost' your baby. On hearing the crying Hilary would think *"So that's where I put him."* She felt guilty but also that she may be losing her mind.

Hilary's daughter was born a year later but her marriage was already close to collapse. They handled the miscarriage very differently. She eventually divorced her husband as *"his disappointment with life was so great, he was unable to let his grief go."* Hilary describes how her husband wasn't adaptable enough to recover from the experience of the death of *"his son"*. She says, *"his grief caused him to throw away a big piece of his life,"* and although he has regular access to his daughter Hilary has since remarried and her daughter now has a stepfather too.

The most positive thing that Hilary did at the time of her bereavement was to turn to the Internet and organisations such as The Miscarriage Association. She called at "*an awful hour of the morning and their librarian answered – she was so sympathetic and helpful. I cried for the first time since the effect of the anaesthetic.*" Hilary got involved with her local branch of the association and received support from others in similar circumstances. She lobbied with the Miscarriage Association and other organisations to reduce the age at which miscarried foetuses were eligible for funeral ceremonies. She tried to persuade her local church to put up a small monument with little pockets for small bunches of violets and daisies. "*It would be a lovely place under a tree – like the tomb to the unknown warrior, but this would be to unknown babies.*" But the council wouldn't allow it, "*it would be too morbid and encourage too many sobbing women.*"

Hilary now imagines her son as a boy a year older than her daughter. The priest at the hospital kept a book that grieving parents could write in. Hilary wrote in the book on the anniversary of her son's birth for eight years. New babies were entered into the book – and when there were so many that she had to turn over the page, she felt she had received a signal that it was time to stop. Hilary stresses the importance of funerals. She strongly believes that the grieving process goes on for much longer in miscarriage when there is no funeral. She regrets the fact that when her gran died her mother decided that funerals were not the place for children so she was not permitted to attend. Hilary now values the significance of the funeral ceremony for everybody to enable them to go through the grieving process.

When Hilary was working with the Miscarriage Association they gave regular talks at hospitals. "*They had nurses there who had miscarried 30 years earlier who sobbed their hearts out because they were suddenly given permission to express their grief. Some of them came to meetings two or three times.*" Hilary extols the advice of the Miscarriage Association that you should "*say it out loud, make it real and then walk away.*" Hilary thinks that in general we don't deal with death terribly well. "*We usually get a pat on the back and a 'there, there, let's get up and get on with it' — unless it's someone like Princess Diana, there's no extended period when we're allowed to grieve. The Princess Diana thing was overdone but we all need space for remembrance.*"

Hilary would like to be remembered for being nice and being liked. She says the biggest lesson she's learned in life is that "*you can't control it, so what you need to do is to keep your heart open. There's bad stuff and good stuff — you just need to be adaptable.*" Hilary would like to be cremated to the sound of loud and heavy rock & roll music (she sings in a band). She'd like everyone to "*get pissed*" and celebrate that she was around and "*cry if you want to too. Don't feel obliged to come if you don't want to, but the piss up and the party will be on me!*"

Although raised in the Church of England Hilary has had enough of organised religion. She believes in God and considers herself a Christian but she's not sure about the afterlife and the God she believes in has no divisions between different religions — Muslims, Protestants, whatever - they are all the same. She values people and her family most and would expect to be remembered by her daughter and her grandchildren.

Her father now suffers from Alzheimer's disease and Hilary believes that this will become one of our biggest social problems. One in ten people over the age of 70 suffer from dementia and Hilary says that these people suffer "*a little death every day.*" How will society manage the problem of babysitting all these people? Hilary points out that in some cases death comes as more of a blessed relief to the extent that the carers feel guilty about it. At the same time she says, "*We have to proactively put some respect, dignity and value into old people, the cult of youth has to shift.*"

Anna had a very special relationship with her elderly aunt. Coming from a dysfunctional family where there was collusion by her mother to cover up her father's physical abuse of Anna, her aunt was the only person who supported her when she dealt with these problems. Whereas Anna's mother would hide things for show her aunt had a similar attitude and outlook to Anna - "*blunt, in your face, up front. She also used to make a good bread pudding when I was a child.*" "*My aunt was a mentor*", says Anna "*offering practical and emotional support and was someone I could visit and talk to whilst I was going through therapy.*" Even though her aunt had been ill for quite some time, nothing prepared Anna (then aged 46) for her aunt's death at the age of 74. Her aunt had suffered from ulcerated legs for the past seven years. She was always in and out of hospital where the conditions left much to be desired and Anna recalls having to find her hearing aid amidst the mould on her nightdress – "*it was like watching someone being tortured.*" Her aunt became bed-ridden and, ten days before she died, one of her legs was amputated. Anna had been to visit her when she started to have panic attacks after the operation but had expected her to recover afterwards. When she later telephoned her aunt's daughter-in-law she was told that her aunt was sitting up in bed eating – and that she was cheerful. On hearing this news Anna decided to leave it until after the weekend to visit the hospital again. Indeed she couldn't work out why someone would be calling her so early on a bank holiday Monday morning. On hearing the news of her aunt's death she felt she should have waited to see her before dying.

Anna broke down and cried for an hour and a half. She had to tell her nephew the news of his great aunt's death but she couldn't drive to see him. She thought she could cope but she couldn't. She tried to fill the space by doing something - so she didn't sit around. Her aunt always prayed to Mary so before the funeral Anna went to church, found a candle and prayed to Mary. Anna eventually became totally consumed with grief to the extent that one of her PR clients thought she was having a breakdown. Anna describes the funeral as *"horrible, though the guy conducting the service was wonderful. I didn't want to see her dead; I'd rather remember her as she was. I didn't want to see her open coffin."* She didn't want to leave the crematorium and eventually had to be removed. Anna had an *"intense feeling, like being joined by a cord"* to her aunt. Anna's aunt had been the person she turned to for advice and support, so now she turned to her boyfriend. Her nephews and nieces were sweet *"they would come and sit on my lap and hug me"* and her clients were *"strangely supportive"* sending her kind messages and putting her under no pressure to get work done immediately. One of her neighbours who used to be a care worker was particularly helpful, taking her to Sainsburys, making sure she ate and telephoning her to make sure she was all right.

Although Anna doesn't believe in heaven or the afterlife, she does believe in spirituality and telepathy which she feels explains an incident that happened after her aunt died. Anna was visiting a garden centre when she noticed one yellow azalea bush which she simply had to buy. It reminded her of the crematorium in Hertfordshire where her aunt's ashes were scattered in a beautiful Japanese garden full of yellow azaleas. Anna bought a number of other plants all of which were much smaller than the beautiful yellow azalea. When she got back to her car, she looked at her receipt and discovered that she had only been charged ten pence for the azalea bush. It made her laugh and she felt it was too much of a coincidence – it was as if her aunt had 'planted' the bush there.

Anna realises that two years on she still has lots of grief. She no longer feels that her aunt is with her, but feelings of being with her aunt when she was alive are still with her. When Anna recently visited Poland (her aunt's husband had been Polish), she had to light a candle in church and had an overwhelming desire just to sob away the pain. Her aunt was a formidable character and it's almost as if Anna felt she had to follow in her footsteps. She has already taken on some of her aunt's traditions such as buying her nephews and nieces selection boxes of sweets for Christmas every year.

Anna talks openly about the psychological damage caused as a result of her father's abuse. The most significant experience of her life was finding out who she was and learning that she wasn't wrong – "*Lots of things happened when I was a kid. I was told that I imagined them, but I didn't. There simply wasn't the evidence to back them up.*" Anna is "*whole again, but damaged now, though I'd be in much more of a mess if my aunt hadn't supported me.*" With no children of her own, Anna likes to support her extended family of three nephews and nieces, two godchildren and eight adopted "*fairy god-children*". She has already had the satisfaction of two of her god-children telling her that she has made a real difference to their lives – one has lived on her own since 15 and the other has been able to become a step-mum with Anna's help and advice.

Anna says she doesn't want to die as there's so much to do - "*gardening, travelling, scuba diving, relationships, seeing how kids turn out.*" However, she keeps a 'death file' in a plastic folder and knows that she would either like to be cremated and thrown out to sea or buried in a wicker coffin on a green burial site with a tree on top. She hasn't decided yet although she's seen a nice red, cardboard coffin. She's even thought of planning a party for everyone when she's dead. She'd like to leave a recording as a posthumous DJ and devote songs to all the people at the funeral. She could get all her jokes in. Her friends thought this idea rather sick and have banned the idea – but she'd still like to pick the tunes played. She'd hope to be remembered until all the people she's known have died – *"for as long as it's useful, to give someone a laugh, or make them feel better. It doesn't matter after that. It would be nice to be remembered for giving happiness and enriching people's lives"*, she adds.

Anna was brought up a Baptist, but had no education about death or dying either at school, or Sunday school. But she had pets – and describes how they held funerals for their goldfish *"Jimmie, John, Paul, George and Ringo, plus various dogs, newts and rabbits."* She explains how no one talked about death in the 60's and 70's. Her grandma was 66 and really fit when Anna, aged nine asked her if she was going to die before her swimming gala in nine months time. *"Grandma's response was that she would do her best to be around for the swimming gala!"* Her own godchildren are already talking about the time when Anna gets old and they can use her wheelchair to *"hide their booze."* Her nephew is positively excited about her *"getting killed"* so he can inherit her dogs. Unfortunately she hasn't organised a will yet but she will be leaving money in trust for her fairy godchildren.

To Anna, bereavement means getting the pain and sadness out, though this is not considered to be very British. If someone young dies it's somehow more acceptable to be emotional - much less so for an older person or, say, a much-loved pet. Yet the feeling inside is still the same. You hear people saying, "*They did very well at the funeral, they held it together.*" British people are expected to bottle up their emotions they are frightened to sob and get over their grief. Anna says she now understands why women from some other cultures are prone to wailing and throwing themselves at coffins. There is a need to mourn; otherwise the loss is simply glossed over.

Abena is one of 17 siblings of a family that originated in Nigeria, though she is British. Her mother died in 1989 from leukaemia, when Abena was 20 years old. Now 37 Abena still vividly remembers the moment she *felt* her mother had died. As she was very ill the nurses at the hospital told Abena to get on with things as normal. She went out shopping with friends when she was over-taken by an urge to go to the hospital – she says she just knew that something was wrong. She called the hospital from the store she was in and made the taxi race from Tottenham Court Road to Hampstead in just 8 minutes. She knew her mother had already died and felt distraught that she hadn't been there. She also felt that by not being there she had let her mother down since she had been ill for around a year. Abena also remembers standing in church and read-ing a passage – it was like a dream. She felt numb not real. She collapsed in floods of tears at the graveside.

Abena says she doesn't feel like a bereaved child any more. Since lots of time has elapsed she's put it past her and moved on. But she still smiles when she thinks of her mum – "*she was my strength and the things she taught me have helped me to deal with different situations and to move forward.*" Abena is, herself, more worried about taxes and unforeseen change than death. "*For many people, a funeral is an opportunity to pay their last respects and say goodbye. Then, after the*

funeral they routinely go to the cemetery and tend to the flowers until they come to a
point when there is no longer any connection to the spirit of the person who has died.
Some people find the rituals of funerals and cemeteries comforting." Abena feels that
her mother's spirit is with her wherever she is. She doesn't particularly want
to have a formal funeral service herself – she would prefer to be cremated, to
have her ashes scattered and for there to be a party for her friends and relatives. She would like a cheap coffin, which she would decorate herself with
photos of all the good times she has had. She'd prefer to spend her money on
a big beach barbeque for all her friends in southern Spain where everyone
could share their tales. Her philosophy of life is that you shouldn't be afraid to
enjoy your life now and that you shouldn't have any regrets.

Abena would like to be remembered as someone who inspired others to
achieve things and brought happiness to people's lives. She's lived her life on
her own terms and achieved all the things she wanted to. She'd like to be
remembered by the people who knew her, as opposed to having her life
recorded in history books – but she'd expect to be remembered as long as
those people are alive. Her mother died feeling sick, stressed and shaking.
Abena now values a peaceful, stress-free life above all else. She runs her own
massage and stress therapy practice to help others be fitter and healthier. She
says that whilst all religions have important values to teach she is not a follow-
er of any one of them. She describes herself as spiritual, not religious, though
she was raised a Christian with a Muslim father. Her mother was very religious
and was ready to '*meet her maker*' when she died, yet she was also afraid to leave
her daughter (for her daughter's sake.) Abena believes in reincarnation – that
the spirit never dies; it remains in the atmosphere or the universe in some
shape or form. Her niece is very much like her mother in her mannerisms and

the things she says – Abena believes her mother lives on in her, the things she does and through her niece.

Marika is a 47-year-old Scandinavian who lost three family members in 2005 – including her 41-year-old English husband who died within 9 months of being diagnosed with colon cancer. Marika feels very badly about the way she was treated by her in-laws at the time of her husband's death. Surprisingly, as others will testify, the way she was overlooked is not uncommon.

Marika, who is herself a survivor of cancer, watched as her husband battled against the disease – he was determined that he could buy himself a cure and eventually went to hospital in the USA where better care was available. She says that he became very angry that no amount of money would save his life. He eventually flew back to his parents' house in Windermere where he died. However it wasn't until two months after his death that Marika received her husband's death certificate in the post. In the intervening time she had desperately tried to get hold of him. Her parents-in-law didn't invite her to the funeral and she didn't even know whether he had been buried or cremated. Marika claims that his parents couldn't cope with the loss of their son – they needed someone to blame – and that was her.

Marika feels that her treatment by her in-laws has been inhumane. She tried to find bereavement counselling but because of the nature of her situation, there was no one to turn to for help. She wrote extensively to her in-laws and saw lots of solicitors but nothing could bring back the chance to attend her husband's funeral – or at least to find out where he was buried or where his ashes are scattered. She said what she wanted to say last year when she bought a card for him and wrote the simple words '*Thank you for shining so brightly in my world*'. She would like to be able to talk to her husband's parents about him but they will not speak to her. "*He lives on in my mind and that's the most important thing,*" says Marika. After her husband's death, Marika suffered two further bereavements – her aunt and her uncle. These were people she loved as a child and when they passed away it was as if her childhood memories returned. She spent her summers in a summerhouse next to the sea. It was the peak time of her childhood when she was looked after by her aunt who saw fun in everything. Her aunt made Marika run through a field with a bull on the way to the local shop so that they would get there more quickly! She has lots of very happy memories of her aunt and of her uncle's subtle sense of humour. They both died from old age so it was a very different situation from that of her husband.

Marika believes that the soul goes on living forever. She meditates every day and values inner peace. Maybe her life could have been easier if she had been invited to her husband's funeral and if she knew where he was laid to rest. As she says "*Life moves on and one gets on with it as best one can.*" She has grown as a human being as a result of her experience, "*and I still have my memories,*" she says.

Archie, now 29, was 27 when his mother died in a car crash at the age of 59. "*She always drove like a maniac and was in a near fatal crash many years ago – it was probably the best way for her to go,*" he says. Archie describes how his mother seemed to get an adrenalin rush from being late – she was always late for everything so everyone always told her to arrive 10 minutes earlier than she was due. "*They used to joke that she'd be late for her own funeral.*"

Joking aside, Archie, who along with his sister was adopted at birth, was totally shocked when he heard about his mother's accident. He says he went into autopilot, going to the bank to get some cash so he could immediately catch the train to be by his mother's side. The thought crossed his mind that she might die but he also knew she'd had crashes before and felt that she was so strong it would simply be a matter of a few years for her to recover. Her last bad accident was when he was six years old – she'd crashed into the back of a digger and was declared dead at one point. Then there were the other cars that were written off during his childhood.

He remembers loads of people being packed into the village church for his mother's funeral. Once they walked into the church it was as if the world stopped for 15-20 minutes. Everyone tried to compose themselves but they were utterly devastated. Archie hasn't had any counselling but is now considering it as his sister found it very helpful. He discussed things with his girlfriend and with a friend whose father had died about six months before his mother.

Archie mostly remembers his mother telling him off – shouting and swearing – his are very visual memories. He feels he is lucky she didn't die until he was in his late 20s and adds, *"In a weird sort of way, it was the sort of death that she might have planned for herself."* The idea of dying doesn't bother Archie but he thinks that funerals are really morbid. Nevertheless, he understands the problems associated with turning them into a wild party. He attended the funeral of a young friend of his who also died in a car crash. They had always said that they would like to have their favourite type of music played at their funeral – his friend's was "jungle" music, which somehow just didn't seem appropriate at the time.

Archie says the most significant things in his life are the fact of being adopted and his mother's death. He still visits her graveside whenever he goes home. He doesn't go to church but believes there is a god and thinks that reincarnation "*is a distinct possibility.*" He also feels it's important to have a biodegradable coffin and is a firm believer in living wills. Archie's ambition is to "*sort out the British railway network.*" If he achieves this it's something he'd like to be remembered for. He thinks that leaving something behind is important and that it's a good idea to let others know how you'd like to be remembered. "*Imagine if James Dean, or Jim Morrison, had talked about their lives and how they'd like to be remembered*", he adds.

Evelyn has already bought a plot of land for her own burial. When her ex-husband died, her son asked her what was going to happen to her so she decided to take action. The first funeral she ever arranged was her mother's. Her mother died at Christmas and the funeral was on New Year's Eve. Her sister had emigrated to Canada so Evelyn didn't have much help with organising the event and all she knew was that her mother wanted a pink rose on her coffin. Her mother had been keen on ballet so Evelyn asked the local funeral director if they could play some music from Swan Lake. The terse response she received was "*Madam, this IS a funeral.*" As it turned out, there were only two tapes of music deemed to be appropriate that hadn't been stolen from the crematorium! A little while after her mother's funeral Evelyn attended another. A lady who had been a healer at a local hospital for alternative therapies for cancer had organised her own funeral. "*It was super, I didn't know you didn't need to have a vicar – she was buried in the garden with all the animals she'd rescued,*" Evelyn explained. Comparing her mother's "*awful funeral*" with how it could be Evelyn decided to take the initiative regarding her own.

In general there is little choice with funerals. Her local burial ground/crematorium in the Wirral has a very negative atmosphere. As Evelyn was arranging her own funeral she wondered why couldn't have it exactly as she wanted? In her search for somewhere pleasant to be buried Evelyn met Donald Boddy, owner and designer of a new remembrance park at Eastham near Chester. She was "*swept away by it*" to such an extent that she now works for Donald, marketing the site and selling plots. The park will offer humanist funerals with a healer on the site. "*There's a happy and positive feeling about the park,*" she enthuses, "*the trees have healing meanings, lovely smells and earth energies. A Chinese Feng Shui master was involved in the site's design and what this offers is really different from a conveyor belt funeral - in most churchyards there's not even any room for burials.*"

Evelyn believes in "*something. There's an overall energy … god, angels, whatever, there's something out there.*" She was brought up Church of England but no longer goes to church, though she still says prayers to whoever's there. . She "*sort of believes*" in reincarnation. A firm believer that there's too much medical intervention, Evelyn is currently finding out about living wills. She's worked in hospitals as a radiographer and has seen people "*in an awful state – if they were a dog they'd put them down.*" When people feel they've got no quality of life left she feels it would be better to just quietly say goodbye.

Evelyn spends quite a lot of time arranging trips for old folk in the flats where she lives. She's the youngest there and arranges all sorts of things - parties, canal and river trips - she even used to run a rambling club for people who were having a second childhood after open-heart surgery. It's nice to do things for other people and have fun at the same time. She has a wonderful son aged 44 who lives with his wife just outside Washington DC and, having travelled the world, now works in nature conservancy. *"I feel sad about the world at the moment,"* says Evelyn, *"looking after your family, tolerance, kindness, thoughtfulness and manners go a long way. They've got it wrong with education and schools about single parent families. Now there's a nurse in each school so that girls can arrange terminations and children can get sex advice. Children aren't children any more."*

Having a son who is abroad Evelyn would like a very quiet, low-key funeral. She wouldn't want a gravestone and with the park so well looked after she's pleased her son wouldn't have to worry about that. She's got a book and she's writing down all her ideas to give to her son – there are also useful phone numbers for everything he should know about her finances. She'd like to have a big party for all her friends. She'll choose her own music – like Sarah Brightman's *Now it's Time to Say Goodbye*. She'll start off with *Morning Has Broken*. She has the silk flowers already made in her wardrobe. She'd like a nice wicker coffin like Tony Banks', draped in greenery. She'd also like to have fireworks but they can't do that because the Eastham site is on the flight path to Liverpool airport. Instead, she'd like butterflies let out around her coffin. *"When someone dies, you normally have four or five days to sort out the funeral, you don't know where to start. People just don't know what's possible,"* she says.

Evelyn would like to be remembered for organising events and helping people - she's done some mad things! She's not afraid of dying. She tends not to think too much about it – it would be nasty to have a bad accident or to go in a revolting way but when it's your time to go that's it. She's so pleased she met Donald as it's *"such a relief to find somewhere nice to be buried."* All she wants to do now is to tell others that they too have a choice. It's also important that she has saved those who will survive her from the hassle of organising her funeral. *"Funerals do matter; often the vicar doesn't know the person who's died which is awful. The humanist funerals I've been to have been wonderful. There's a mother and daughter team who do them, with beautiful voices, a knowledge of the family and the person who's died, there's a calm atmosphere and everyone is left feeling satisfied, left feeling really good."*

Evelyn's friends think she's completely mad. She makes them laugh. *"Perhaps I'm a bit of an exhibitionist who wants to make a statement, to have something special and different,"* she says, *"but it's also for my son. Not everybody wants to talk about these things. It's amazing how many people don't know what their parents or family want, even if they are very ill – it leaves you with a sense of guilt. People don't die at home now like they used to. You have all sorts of feelings when someone dies – mostly you wish things had been done differently. I'm going to make sure no one feels like that about me."*

Esther Ranzten recently made a programme for BBC2 called *How to Have a Good Death*. She confirmed that two-thirds of the population have never discussed their final wishes with any of their family or friends. She proposed that detailed discussion and the writing of a living will could be a real support for families and friends in *"those dark hours when they are desperate to do the right thing."* Yet even the medical professionals *"shrink from the subject."*

From the ordinary person in the street, to the world-famous celebrity, we all have similar stories of bereavement to tell. Simon Callow, himself the subject of a funeral in *Four Weddings and a Funeral*, told *The Mail on Sunday* about his grandmother's funeral. *"She was an extraordinarily expansive and somewhat eccentric woman. One of her great obsessions was her funeral. She planned it even more metic-*

ulously than Churchill's state funeral. Every day she would add another piece of music that she wanted, until it ended up running to more than seven hours. In the end, of course, in the ghastly and arbitrary way of these things, she died rather unexpectedly. There was a dreadful funeral in a terrible church somewhere. Everyone thought the priest was drunk but he'd actually suffered a stroke. It was just awful, everyone laughed. There was no music, and I was absolutely furious." A little while later, Callow was banned from his partner's funeral by his partner's mother. Another unsatisfactory experience of death. For his own funeral, Callow would like a service filled with solemn music by Sibelius with readings from the Bible and Bhagavad-Gita. He adds "*I would hope that everybody would get profoundly drunk afterwards.*"

When Sarah Smith lost her mother after a helicopter crash she too found the funeral distressing. "*I was petrified the pallbearers would slip my mother out onto the church path. I didn't like the way a fly kept buzzing around the coffins. I kept trying to picture what my mother's body must be like nearly a month after the crash,*" she explained in *The Sunday Times*. "*The morning after the funeral the undertaker delivered a plastic pot filled with her ashes. When we scattered them I assumed they'd be made up of some light dust that would be carried off by the wind just like I'd seen in films. Unfortunately the granules resembled cat litter and there was a lot of it. When some ash got under my fingernails I didn't know what to do - I felt so guilty watching bits of my mother get washed down a plughole.*" Sarah found it helpful speaking to others who had lost a parent and was glad to have had bereavement counselling - "*my weekly hour-long sessions gave me the space to truly grieve, as well as taking the pressure off friends and family, and stopping me worry that I'd become a death bore.*"

Esther Rantzen wishes she had talked to her parents and her husband about their deaths instead of avoiding the subject, fearing they would be hurt or distressed. She also suggests that hospitals should be made to be more sensitive to the importance of the precious last moments of life. As she says *"only by facing the fact that we are all mortal can we achieve what we most want for ourselves and those we love, a good death, the final celebration of a great life."*

When I discovered that my father-in-law had terminal lung cancer I suggested that my mother-in-law read a couple of books. One of them was *The Tibetan Book of Living and Dying*. I wasn't sure if, as a rather puritanical Christian she would actually get around to reading it but I felt it would be helpful to anyone – especially the part about saying goodbye. It simply says to imagine yourself standing by the bed of the person you love and saying with the deepest and most sincere tenderness: *"I am here with you and I love you. You are dying, and that is completely natural, it happens to everyone. I wish you could stay here with me, but I don't want you to suffer any more. The time we have had together has been enough, and I shall always cherish it. Please no don't hold onto life any longer. Let go. I give you my heartfelt permission to die. You are not alone, now or ever. You have all my love."*

Experiences from the Developing World

Death in Zambia

Douglas J Davis says the *"One of the tragedies of today's world is that death is treated as a cause of concern in some contexts while in others the warfare and sickness killing millions pass practically unnoticed."* He adds that the relative worth of life differs, not least in terms of how the media decide to comment or not.

So what happens when people die in a developing country? I travelled to Zambia in south-central Africa to find out more:

MORTALITY AND AIDS :

In the developed world no one expects to die of dysentery, cholera or malaria, let alone tuberculosis or AIDS. Some of these illnesses such as AIDS are treatable with expensive combinations of antiretroviral drugs and others have been completely eradicated. In Western Europe for instance the number of people living with AIDS continues to increase. There were an estimated 2,252 deaths there in 2004 and 115,000 people living with HIV.

Sub-Saharan Africa is the region of the world most affected by HIV and AIDS. An estimated 25.8 million people were living with HIV at the end of 2005 and approximately 3.1 million new infections occurred during that year. In the past year the epidemic has claimed the lives of an estimated 2.4 million people in this region and more than 12 million children have been orphaned by the disease. National HIV prevalence rates vary greatly between countries – in Somalia and Gambia the prevalence is under 2% of the adult population whereas in South Africa and Zambia, around 20% of the adult population is infected. In four southern African countries the national adult HIV prevalence rate has risen higher than was thought possible and now exceeds 24% - these are Botswana (37.3%), Lesotho (28.9%), Swaziland (38.8%) and Zimbabwe (24.6%).

The extent of the AIDS epidemic in Africa is only now becoming clear as increasing numbers of people with HIV become ill. In the absence of massively expanded efforts of prevention, treatment and care by Western governments and pharmaceutical companies, the AIDS death toll in the African continent is expected to continue rising before peaking at around the end of the decade. This means that the worst impact of the epidemic on these societies is still to be felt over the course of the next ten years and beyond. Its social and economic consequences are already being widely felt, not only in health, but in education, industry, agriculture, transport and human resources.

In the developing world where 95% of new global HIV infections occur, most of those infected are doomed to a gruesome and painful death. Those who find a place in a hospital are fortunate since all available beds are filled with the dead and the dying. There are almost no drugs to treat painful opportunistic infections let alone the virus itself. *"I want to know what you worry about,"* asks the teacher of a Grade 5 LIFE SKILLS class at an Elementary School in Harare, Zimbabwe. She asks the children to write about their greatest worry on a piece of paper, gathers them all up and asks each of the children to talk about what it is that most concerns them. In seven out of every ten instances the words on the paper have something to do with death: the death of a parent, of a sibling, of an aunt, uncle of a friend, or a friend's father. When the teacher asked the children what they could do about this all-pervasive death they answered *"pray."* The teacher explained to Stephen Lewis, former Canadian ambassador to the UN who now writes for *The Toronto Globe and Mail, "when everyone is dying all around you, the children don't know what to do but pray. We pray after school, we pray at lunch-breaks, and we pray on Saturdays, we pray all the time. For the children, since nothing else seems to work, the intervention of God is the only hope left."*

Zambia's problems since the mid 1980's have been compounded by one of the most devastating HIV and AIDS epidemics. The Republic of Zambia is a large country at the heart of sub-equatorial Africa. More than a quarter of its 10.5-11 million people live in two urban areas near the centre: in the capital Lusaka and in the industrial towns of the Copperbelt. The rest of the country is very sparsely populated and the majority of the people make their living as subsistence farmers. Independent for the past four decades, it is a peaceful country but also one of the poorest and least developed nations on earth and has crippling debt. Around two-thirds of the population lives on less than a dollar a day. Added to this, one in every six adults in Zambia is living with HIV. In 2003, 89,000 of its inhabitants died of AIDS. There are now approximately 630,000 AIDS orphans and life expectancy has fallen below 40 years.

HIV has spread throughout Zambia and to all sections of society. However some groups are particularly vulnerable – most notably young women and girls. AIDS has worst hit those in their most productive years and, as families have disintegrated, thousands have been left destitute. The impact of AIDS has gone far beyond thelevel of household and community. All areas of the public sector and the economy have been weakened and national development has been stifled.

In Zambia most HIV infections are the result of unprotected heterosexual sex. Many thousands of sexual transmissions could be avoided if people consistently used condoms. However for a lot of people to do this would involve overcoming substantial practical, cultural or religious obstacles. Most non-sexually transmitted HIV infections are passed from mother to child. Without access to preventative drugs nearly 40% of HIV-positive mothers give birth to infected babies. An estimated 30,000 infants contract the virus each year in Zambia whether during pregnancy, at the time of birth, or while breast-feeding. Most of these children die before they are 5 years old. Around half of all transmissions during pregnancy and birth could be avoided if every mother received a single dose of antiretroviral treatment.

Gender inequality also hampers HIV prevention efforts. As in many other parts of the world men traditionally play the dominant role in most relationships while women and girls are expected to be submissive. Females also have less access to education and the mass media. As a result women can lack the confidence, skills and knowledge necessary to negotiate safe relationships with men and to make independent lifestyle choices. A woman is usually taught that she must obey her husband and that it is wrong to refuse sex with him. Less than two-thirds of adults (of either gender) believe that a woman can refuse sex if she suspects her husband has HIV. Various aspects of traditional Zambian culture also make women more vulnerable to HIV infection. Among these is "sexual cleansing" a common ritual in which a deceased man's relative has sex with his widow in the belief that this will dispel evil forces. The HIV status of the people involved is not always taken into consideration. Alternative, risk-free rituals do however exist and are becoming popular in some areas. Many of the most tragic stories connected with HIV transmission involve the sexual abuse of children. The high prevalence of HIV has increased the level of sexual violence and coercion not least because some of the victims are vulnerable AIDS orphans. Men are targeting increasingly younger sexual partners whom they assume to be HIV-negative and the "virgin cure" myth (which claims that sex with a virgin can cure AIDS) fuels much of this abuse. Orphans who inform against their guardians risk either abandonment or punishment or totally insensitive treatment in the hands of the local police department.

There is also the problem of a transient population where truck drivers and seasonal workers such as fishermen engage in short term relationships and so-called temporary marriages. Sex workers, women and girls involved in cross-border trading, and the poor are particularly vulnerable. Prisoners are also at high risk especially from homosexual sex which is common practice though officially illegal. Yet the government still refuses to lift its ban on distributing condoms to prisoners.

As HIV can be sexually transmitted it is often presumed that those who are living with the virus have brought the disease upon themselves by having many sexual partners and moral judgements are made. Women are especially vulnerable to this prejudice and are often blamed for infecting their children. Victims of the stigma suffer physical and social isolation from their family, friends and community. They are made to feel guilty, ashamed and inferior. Those who fear becoming stigmatised are usually unwilling to volunteer for an HIV test. The very fact of purchasing condoms or discussing safer sex may be seen as an indication of infection and lead to stigmatisation. People who know or suspect that they are HIV-positive are generally reluctant to reveal their status even to their partners and family or to come forward for treatment. Tragically some of the worst discrimination occurs in clinics and hospitals. Patients known or suspected to have HIV are sometimes given very low priority and may be subjected to degrading treatment or breaches of confidentiality – at worst they may even be denied drugs and treatment. When the male head of a family dies it is common for his entire property to be seized by his relatives leaving his widow and children with nothing. Many abandoned children live in big cities where they survive by begging, stealing and prostitution. It is projected that the number of AIDS orphans in Zambia could rise to 974,000 by 2014.

The prevalence of HIV and AIDS in Zambia has a huge effect on every aspect of life and on the nation's economy. As far as healthcare is concerned, more than 50% of hospital beds are filled by patients with AIDS related illnesses. The cost of caring for these people is relatively expensive, leaving fewer funds to help those suffering from other ailments. There is a lack of drugs, equipment and personnel in this sector of the economy and the physical infrastructure of hospital buildings is deteriorating. AIDS also has an impact on education. Many children do not attend school because a parent or guardian is suffering from or has died from AIDS. Only two thirds of primary school age children and less than a quarter of those aged 14-18 years attend school regularly. Teachers are also in short supply as a result of the epidemic. In general employment according to the Zambian Business Coalition 82% of known causes of employee deaths are HIV related and 17% of those recruited are replacement staff for those who have died or left due to HIV-related infections. AIDS kills people in their prime of life stripping the workforce of valuable skills and experience and leaving fewer people to teach the next generation. In agricultural areas, the loss of a few workers at the crucial periods of planting and harvesting can significantly reduce the size of the harvest. Lack of food and poor nutrition makes HIV-positive people more vulnerable to infections and hastens the progress of AIDS. In short, AIDS is the key contributor to the vicious circle of poverty in Zambia.

Over the years a wide range of media have been used to carry messages about AIDS and children have been taught the biological facts in school. Basic awareness has been raised but many misconceptions remain. Although almost all adult Zambians know that HIV/AIDS exists, 11% of men and 19% of women still don't know that it can be avoided. Nearly a quarter of adults think that mosquitoes can transmit HIV; one in five think they can be infected by witchcraft and 12% believe that sharing a meal with an infected person can put them at risk. The level of knowledge is lower in rural areas than in towns and women are less knowledgeable than men.

The role of condoms in curbing the spread of Zambia's AIDS epidemic has been a subject of prolonged controversy in this mainly Christian nation. Increasing the availability of condoms has been a key part of national policy since the mid-1980s and the Health Department aims to distribute some 25 million condoms each year (in a country of 5 million adults). However, many church leaders and politicians claim that condoms cause promiscuity and immorality and they have opposed any promotional campaigns for this reason. Near the end of his presidency former president Frederick Chiluba said, " *I don't believe in condoms myself because it is a sign of weak morals on the part of the user ...the only answer is abstinence.*" Chiluba's statements were widely condemned by AIDS activists and NGOs. However the government of his successor Levy Mwanawasa has expounded the same moral arguments and even went so far as to ban the distribution of condoms in schools – a decision endorsed by the head of the National AIDS Council, Mosemay Musonda. In 2001 much to the dismay of foreign donors including USAID, UNAIDS and the World Bank, a series of television advertisements that promoted condom use were taken off the air after generating countless letters of protest. It was widely suspected that the president had personally intervened to initiate the ban. The USAID-funded Zambia Social Marketing Project reported that condom sales more than doubled from 4.7 million in 1993 to 10.6 million in 2002. However the use of condoms remains very infrequent especially in rural areas where a village may be miles from the nearest sales outlet. Education efforts have had less impact in rural areas where men retain the traditional position of authority and women believe that they are unable to negotiate safer sex. The decline in HIV prevalence among some young women suggest that prevention campaigns may be starting to work though it's clear that stigma, gender inequality and opposition to condoms remain deeply entrenched. The number of people living with HIV is likely to continue to rise significantly due to the more widespread use and free availability of drugs.

FUNERALS:

There are great differences in Zambia between burials in tribal villages and those carried out in town. In villages there is no refrigeration so bodies must be buried by the day following death at the latest. There is no time for any extended family to make their way to the burial and indeed most of the family are also members of the tribe and live close by. A runner is sent to notify everybody of the death. The body is usually wrapped in a blanket and sometimes timber from old furniture is used to make a box. Each tribe has its own traditions for burying the dead. There are seven major tribes each with its own language, culture and physique and 72 minor tribes with regional differences in dialect, culture and community.

In towns a funeral starts with an announcement of the death through government free media such as the sponsored radio programme *Call Personal Messages*, broadcast in English as well as the seven main languages of Zambia. The body can be kept refrigerated for up to four days after death whilst waiting for the arrival of relatives. Guests might spend several days at the house of the deceased enjoying the family's hospitality at their expense – an arrangement that is often abused by guests who are often after as much free food and drink as they can get. Tents are often erected outside the house to accommodate all the visitors who spend nights around a bonfire. As there is generally a shortage of available transport, open-topped trucks are hired to ferry the guests to the cemetery.

The corpse is then washed by family members, as a preparation for burial. Recently, the trend has also been for young people to go to cemeteries to earn money to wash the bodies of people they didn't even know. This is frowned upon by the older generation, as children weren't even allowed to see bodies before, let alone freely touch the dead. Wooden caskets are the preferred form of coffin and families will go to extreme lengths to ensure that sufficient funds are collected for an appropriate coffin. It would take years to re-educate people that a bamboo coffin is better for the environment and a more sensible use of resources than burying their money. However in recent years people have begun to talk more openly about cemeteries and death, largely due to the influence of overseas cemetery operators and designers coming to Lusaka to help solve the problem of dealing with the enormous number of bodies. Tombstones are very expensive, rarely placed on graves and, if they are, are not usually engraved – in fact the lettering used for memorials is often stolen. The burden of having to support funeral expenses is also borne by the community through acquaintances that might have developed over time such as members of a local church. In many cases churches have a 'funeral fund' from contributions made every Sunday to meet the needs of those who cannot meet even the most basic funeral expenses.

There are three main cemeteries in Lusaka. In Lusaka, graveyards define status. An old graveyard will count dignitaries such as politicians, civil leaders, wealthy families and local celebrities among its buried. Such cemeteries, though officially full, may still be open to those with funds available to bury their dead. Zarina Geloo, a Zambian journalist, recounted the contrasting funerals of two friends who both had AIDS. One was a high profile business-man whose service was *"an austere, expensive affair,"* presumably organised by funeral directors whom only the rich can hope to afford. His wife also managed to secure a burial spot in one of Lusaka's oldest cemeteries. This man's funeral was a subdued affair where there wasn't even a hint that he had died of AIDS.

The other funeral that Zarina attended was total mayhem. His desperately poor family couldn't find a suitable spot in one of the overcrowded cemeteries so decided to cremate him. Only a handful of workmates and family made up the cortege. At the crematorium relatives fought about who had taken what from his house during the wake. Zarina explains that there are two societies that exist in Zambia: The 30% of rich politicians, business people and employees of international organisations - where the stigma against AIDS, and embarrassment, is so deep that they will travel to neighbouring counties for

HIV tests and medication. The other 70%, who live in townships on the periphery of the city, "*know about AIDS and talk about it quite candidly, but their immediate concern is the next meal... they expect to die, you don't have to tell them that they will die from AIDS.*"

One of the main cemeteries in Lusaka is a free cemetery available to the poor and known as the AIDS graves. The largest cemetery is Leopards Hill and it extends for miles. It consists of unkempt land where, if tombstones exist, they are hidden in long grass and overgrown vegetation that is inhabited by snakes – among them the second most venomous and fastest moving snake in the world, the black mamba. Dissected by dusty tracks that become awash with mud during the rainy season, the cemetery is a dangerous place to visit alone. Guests gather for a funeral, the numbers attending usually averaging around 100-150 and often arriving in huge articulated lorries. There will be a place to view the coffin and much wailing takes place before the coffin is buried. My guide informs me that many of the women present are "*professional wailers*"! The gravediggers seem to be acting rather furtively. They prefer to dig in the evening or early in the morning so they are not seen as there is even a stigma attached to being a gravedigger. Some other workers grouped together around a steaming pot are selling compost to put on top of the graves. Apparently they are cooking something that looks like a squirrel though it may actually be a rat. Most of the most recent graves are mounds of earth with no identification apart from a number. The numbers of older graves have either had their markers or tombstones stolen, or are lost amidst a sea of long grass and weeds. There is hardly any space left in this huge cemetery where the roads seem to go on forever so people have started to bury the dead on the roads themselves. This cemetery will be totally full within the next couple of months and there will be no other free burial space available.

The old Leopards Hill cemetery is slightly different. This is a city council cemetery where payment must be made for space. The cemetery was originally built by Europeans living in the area and the first part of the cemetery is much better laid out with quite a few gravestones and monuments in evidence. The area is still very overgrown and becomes much less organised further away from the area first used for burials. There are few spaces left here and burials must be made between existing graves. There is a huge amount of rubbish and vandalism in evidence, as well as more overgrown vegetation, making it difficult to see where the graves are. Many of the names and lettering have been removed from tombstones and sometimes the graves themselves have been raided for the coffins and anything else of value that might be inside. The practice of putting concrete on top of graves has become a popular way of preventing thieves gaining access, but there are no guards here to ensure the security of these final resting places. Even a large memorial to the victims of a plane crash has had the tiles removed from its cover. The cemetery is in desperate need of restoration – something that a charity called New Leaf has made proposals for.

Another free cemetery, Chilenje (formerly Mpoloto), which is now disused, was such a popular hiding place for thieves that the land has already been flattened to make way for redevelopment. New Leaf charity is hoping to restore this for use as a children's park. However, there is competition to use the land for commercial purposes such as industrial, retail or private housing. In 2004 Brown Mwambanya, a director of the New Leaf Charity, visited the UK to address the annual seminar of the Confederation of Burial Authorities on the

Zambian burial crisis and raise support for restoration work. He also spent three weeks touring British cemeteries to see how they are operated and maintained. New Leaf's aims and objectives are first to create partnership and sustainable action programmes to restore and maintain existing cemeteries including those that are disused. And second to provide bereavement care and support services linked with educational, training and employment programmes. According to Brown, New Leaf is the first non-governmental organisation to address the social issues arising from the current cemetery crisis throughout the seventy two districts of Zambia.

In his speech Brown said, *"We see ourselves taking responsibility to co-ordinate, manage and implement change within our cemeteries, starting in our capital city Lusaka. Cemeteries there are in a deplorable state. People talked into participating in our surveys wondered if my management team and I were of sound mind to even contemplate such a task and if we really understood the size of the mountain we were intending to climb. We are aware of the size of the problem, we are prepared to undertake the challenge and we are convinced that lookng after the Gardens of Remembrance for departed souls is a noble task. In every journey throughout life you have to take one step at a time towards your journey's end and this is the first step of a very long and hard journey."*

Finally, we go to see the spectacular site for a new private cemetery on 800 acres of land in the Chamba Valley which is owned by a local farmer. The developer of the site has been informed that the city, which is now burying around 2,500 per month will run out of burial space in two months and that panic is about to set in. However there is a lot to be done before the cemetery will be operational. They have to build five kilometres of new road over soft ground, divert a major sewage channel, build new culverts, upgrade another five kilometres of existing road, alter a major roundabout, mark out 30,000 graves and build long stretches of internal roads and a building facility, as well as running five km of security electric fencing (there will be two electric fences with 24 hour security guards and guard dogs patrolling in between), drill two water boreholes, run electricity to the site, create a major drainage and irrigation system, not to mention the recruiting and training of 400 staff. The ultimate aim is for this site to have space for 300,000 graves with a capacity for 100 burials each day – on average, one every five minutes. It is envisaged that the cemetery will last for about 10 years until it reaches full capacity and will have around a million visitors a year.

Due to AIDS, Zambia is forecast to have a high number of orphans and, in a culture where family roots are important and frequently passed down by oral tradition, one unique feature of this new cemetery will be its use of the Internet in conjunction with the digital time capsule, www.diaryofmankind.com to help families and communities record their history.

The cemetery is to be designed to meet Zambian cultural and religious requirements whilst being operated and maintained to European standards. By providing a secure environment families are able to visit and maintain graves and honour the memory of their loved ones in ways we take for granted. Zambian business people are already seeing opportunities for new support businesses including the provision of memorials and horticulture.

Brown Mwambanya and Chande Kapundu, a Zambian artist, designer and businessman held an exhibition and Insaka at Lusaka's National Museum to create public debate, highlight the burial crisis and discuss new ideas. Lusaka was originally developed as a Garden City and Chande is creating an annual garden festival to encourage people to restore Lusaka to its Garden City status and for people once again to take pride in their national and family heritage including their parks and cemeteries.

In the meantime there will be an opportunity for charities and individuals to sponsor burial plots, trees and landscaped gardens, thereby giving others a chance to be remembered. The cemetery will also be promoted as a template for other African governments. Officials will be invited to see what is being done, learn about the training schemes and employment structures for the burial ground.

In the wake of the AIDS crisis, Zambians are also being encouraged to look at cremation as a burial option. However, Zambians are by nature a very superstitious people who fear changes in cultural practices and thus far there are no modern cremation facilities in Zambia other than by log fire. If a person has not gone through the burial rites and is not settled, any misfortune that befalls the surviving family members will be attributed to the dead person's "*wandering spirit*". It is also a Zambian tradition to construct shrines at burial sites. Zarina Geloo suggests that people will simply have to be prepared to travel further to graveyards, since cremation is totally alien to them. In some cases, though, necessity has prevailed, and Zambians are already cremating. Theresa Mukambe, a lecturer at the School of Education, whose mother was cremated said, "*Do we really want valuable land that can be used for development to be taken up by graves? At the rate we are dying, three quarters of Zambia will be a graveyard. Besides I do not think I would want my mother buried in a place where everyone died from AIDS. The body is just a vessel of the spirit, it is only the body that you dispose of because it is useless once the spirit has left it."* Fisho Mwale, the former mayor of Lusaka has also explained that burial rituals can still be performed – in church, at home, on the banks of the river or wherever ashes can be scattered or kept. Ramesh Patel, a Hindu, who heads the only crematorium in Lusaka, says *"I think that there are people who see the value of cremation and there is a sense of closure when bodies are cremated, unlike in burials where one views the dead as alive and resting among other dead."*

BEREAVEMENT AND IMMORTALITY:

The poorest in Zambia construct their dwellings from whatever material is available to them. In tribal villages, huts are made from mud and straw or branches. In the townships some are fortunate enough have concrete, bricks or breezeblocks to use for building. Others must make do with plastic sheeting, corrugated iron, mud and vegetation. Most families, however large, share one main room. Those who are lucky have a television – these being usually very small, black and white and with a grainy picture – it's like going back to the 1960s. CD players and computers are rare commodities. Internet cafes, where available, tend to be in the large shopping arcades frequented almost exclusively by expatriates and very wealthy Zambians.

Zambians are generally well presented and very house-proud. One family I visited had six children aged between 6 and 22 years old. The older girls wore makeup and dressed just like young people in wealthy countries, but they seemed much more polite. Perhaps this is due to the enormous influence of the church in this country. In most of the houses I saw religious pictures, artefacts and inspirational sayings taking pride of place alongside chest freezers and household cleaning equipment. In one, tea was served in a ceremonial manner from an early 1970's earthenware coffee pot that wouldn't have looked out of place in a modernist style London apartment. Photograph albums are usually close to hand and passed proudly to visitors for viewing.

I meet **Salome**, a retired civil servant in her fifties, who is the second of seven siblings, three girls and four boys of whom she is now the sole survivor. The first died in 1961 when she was young and Salome doesn't know the cause of death. One brother died of asthma, another brother was found dead – he'd possibly been drinking too much. A sister died of bronchitis after an operation for tonsillitis - they found she had sores inside her neck. Another had pancreatitis – Salome thinks the cause was something to do with HIV, as she had started to take some drugs though by then it was too late. Her father and mother both died from asthma and her son must have inherited something similar as he doesn't stop sneezing. She has had five children herself one of whom died from tonsillitis at eleven, leaving her with two boys and two girls. She is very saddened by her son's sneezing complaint and wonders why this should happen to her. It makes her cry and her only consolation is from the priest who comforts her with the words of God. She says *"there are so many problems, so many questions unanswered, but sometimes we have to have a challenge, to have bad things happen, things happen for a reason."*

Salome is also the guardian of two children orphaned by her last sister's death and two left by her brother. Her cousin and her cousin's husband died too, so she's also looking after their daughter. In 1971 Salome's husband was stabbed by a student while he was at university and she was expecting her third child. He's now disabled and uses a wheelchair. To help overcome her enormous sense of loss Salome talks to her children. Her daughters, in particular, are very close to her. One has three children and her *"big son"* has two children – they're all married. The children she now looks after include two twenty year olds, as well as children of thirteen, fourteen and fifteen years, plus five grandchildren. She needs four loaves of bread for breakfast and at least two chickens for a good meal – though most of the time they eat millet or maize. It's also a real struggle to pay for educating them all.

Salome's experience of funerals is that they are very expensive. Mourners come to stay until the deceased is buried and they need to be fed. Fortunately, it's not possible to keep the bodies for a long time and even where mortuaries have fridges, they're usually not working, so burial usually takes place the day after someone has died – or a maximum of three days afterwards. Sometimes there's a problem finding the money for a coffin. Her relatives are buried in a number of different cemeteries but she knows where they all are. The graves are usually numbered but occasionally the numbers have been stolen. She managed to buy a tombstone for her son's grave but otherwise these are generally too expensive and few people can afford them. If she had the means Salome would like to provide for better funerals, *"you have to accept that death is a constant, one day it will be me, I am the only one left,"* she says. Salome would like to have a Christian funeral with a church service. She'd like to have singing and hope her friends would choose some songs that she liked. Salome whose sitting room is proudly and prominently adorned with statues and pictures of Jesus and Mary attends church every week and belongs to the Catholic Women's League. They do church work and have a mass every Tuesday. When she's buried, Salome will be buried in the customary manner of the Catholic Women's League – they'll clean her body, tie her veil in a certain way – she'll be wearing her Women's League uniform and holding a copy of their constitution in her right hand.

Salome recalls her past and says, *"When I was a child, there weren't so many deaths as today. We were told that when a body was passing by we should stand still whilst the body was being removed. Nowadays children are so used to seeing bodies, they wave at funeral processions. Younger people have a lack of respect; they don't take funerals seriously, probably because people are dying every day. It's important to have a nice coffin as a last mark of respect. A decent coffin will cost around 500,000 kwachas (almost £100) if it's made of wood. These days many people can't even afford a coffin and carry the body on nothing more than a reed mat."*

Salome realised that her experience of bereavement was not unique and decided that she wanted to help others in a similar situation. She has trained as a counsellor and has helped set up an NGO to provide a community-based counselling organisation known as COBACO. The main aim is to help those affected by bereavement, whether they be orphans, widows or widowers. There will be a free telephone-based, psycho-social counselling service run by volunteers to help those suffering from stress and depression – depression is often cited as a cause of death in Zambia. There will also be a programme to train those newly widowed in basic skills such as tailoring, baking and gardening to enable them to generate an income and eke out an existence without being dependent upon others. Salome's house is being converted into an office equipped to house staff for training and a new house is being built to the rear of the existing premises.

There is tremendous pressure upon extended families and the social system to provide growing numbers of AIDS orphans with appropriate care, resources and supervision. COBACO will seek to address the problem by providing funds for education and advice on nutritional and population issues. I notice that the business plan outlining the costs of the venture has only allowed for the educational sponsorship of ten children. These will be the lucky few since child-headed households have become common, along with child labour, child abuse, the prevalence of "street children" and a general inability for orphans to access education and health care. Many of these young orphans turn to crime. A large number of them eventually end up in prison compounds which are totally lacking in facilities. They don't even have mattresses to sleep on. Salome would like to see the prisoners trained in basic skills too; they could do something useful, like making bamboo coffins and mattresses. Giving them some form of training would reduce the tendency to re-offend when the prisoners are released; otherwise they simply have no future.

The next day I am taken to visit some townships. We travel through Mandevu, a compound inhabited by Zimbabwean settlers. You can tell they are Kore Kore from Zimbabwe because the children are dressed in white. They have a big problem with garbage disposal in this area. We move on to Chipata compound. This is high-density, unplanned settlement on land that was originally used for agricultural purposes. Many of the settlers have come from the former mining areas of the Copperbelt looking for work in Lusaka. Local town and country planning officers have sold the settlers land that they were not authorized to sell and put the takings into their own pockets.

On the way, we pass many small shops where people sell anything they can grow, make or get hold of to keep alive. The shops are basically tables, some with any sort of cover that can be found, arranged haphazardly along the side of dust tracks that pass for roads. Building materials such as sand and stones are simply piled up for sale along the side of the road. A sizeable group of women and children sit atop a huge mound of black charcoal dust – apparently useful for protecting properties against unwanted bugs, amongst other things. The dusty and pot-holed roads are liberally lined with garbage. At some points this has clearly been left to accumulate in the manner of a public rubbish tip except that it's just at the side of the road and it smells rotten. There are lots of children everywhere some working with their parents by the roadside, others are alone, playing or simply hanging around. One thing that's apparent is that none of these children is at school.

I meet 60-year-old **Ruth** who is a typical settler in this area. She came with her husband who had worked in the mines to find somewhere to settle in Zambia. He had a big job at the mines, but was involved in an accident resulting in a sore on his leg that never healed. He was in hospital for a couple of months but eventually died of a heart attack. Two years ago, her 31-year-old eldest daughter who was never married also died. They are both buried together at Leopards Hill without a tombstone. She was worried about being able to feed people at the funerals. It was not the end she would have wanted for either of them. One of her daughters got pregnant at the age of fourteen and is now expecting another child. A further daughter is also pregnant and a third is deaf and dumb. Her son Patrick is at college. Ruth managed to find the capital to set up a Kantemba, a small shop, but life has been very difficult and there have been times when they have all cried together because there hasn't been enough food to eat. Her children couldn't go to school and she had no one to turn to for help. "*As long as I live, my father in heaven will help me and look after me and tell me what to do,*" she says.

Having trained for two and a half years as a nurse, Ruth is a well-educated woman with good communication skills and valuable knowledge to impart to others. She decided that she wanted to help orphaned children and now works in association with the Community Based Counselling Organisation, COBA-CO. She has become very concerned about the amount of crime. She would like to help young people who *"roam in the streets. I worry for the families who don't have God, those who spend their time smoking dagga (marijuana) and drinking beer. At night people come to steal so I put bars on my windows inside and outside. Sometimes they come with an axe to get in. Sometimes they come with guns and take everything."* Ruth believes that social education, particularly the education of women, is the solution to the problem: *"Women can be empowered and educated by counselling to know what is right in society, then there won't be any crime. It's the women who bring up the children – they are the key to the family and they should be teaching their children useful skills, rather than drinking beer. Some women are given gifts by God: they know how to knit, or to make pottery. The local skills of the arts and crafts people are very important – we shouldn't let our culture die out."*

In the townships, Ruth explains, the problems are different from in the villages. The men are generally okay, if they have jobs, but when they get to the age of 50-55, there is nothing for them to do and they are just left to die, that is if they haven't already died from AIDS. It is due to social education that the practice of "cleansing" (where the male inheritor of a dead man's estate has sex with his widow) is less prevalent in town than in the villages. However estates are often still grabbed by relatives sometimes including taking on the wife of the deceased for so long as may be necessary to gain access to her land, property and worldly possessions. Ruth has noticed how young people have changed: "*It used to be taboo for a very young girl to get pregnant, but now it doesn't seem to matter. You see now that children envy other people, they will even become prostitutes just to get the things that they want. This is because their parents aren't telling them how to behave, they have rebelled ... they aren't God-fearing any more.*"

Ruth is a testament to her own Christian morals maintaining high standards of responsibility not only to her direct family but to others too. The same high standards are reflected in her smartly dressed appearance and the fact that the one tiny main room of her house - though very basic - is spotless. A small black and white television flickers in the background. Cleaning materials such as brooms, buckets and mops take pride of place on a large table in the corner of the room. She proudly shows us photographs of her family and introduces us to relatives who are present. On the way out she shows us the communal pit latrine. It's about 50 yards from the house and consists of a hole in the ground surrounded by breezeblocks on three sides. There's no roof. I don't ask how many people use this facility, but there's certainly no means of stopping any passer by from using it. Zambia's high prevalence of dysentery and cholera are a direct result of water pollution and inadequate sanitation – and these dual factors also contribute towards the undermining of sustainable development.

Ruth has helped to set up a small local community within the COBACO called Kabanana so named because it used to be a banana plantation. The community consists of people who can't afford their own homes, widows, orphans and vulnerable children. Lots of these people are illiterate and lack the skills and education to earn a living. Nevertheless, the group consisting largely of women has already constructed a road themselves. The Kabanana community has a small office and a garden where they meet to discuss their problems and learn new skills to help them become self-sufficient. I am greeted by a group of around 30 women, men and older children singing and dancing in my honour – a very moving and humbling experience.

They start their meeting with a prayer, apparently to thank me for helping them. I have a wind-up radio to present to their group and it has been negotiated that I'll pay each of the thirty people present 5,000 kwachas (about one pound sterling) each. We write down the names of all those in attendance as a precautionary measure but somehow after a few minutes the list has already crept up to over 50 people as more hear of my visit and come to join the proceedings. Is this what international development organisations mean by trade facilitation I wonder? They all want to tell me their stories. Stories of sadness - stories of death after death after death.

First I talk to **Elizabeth** a widow with five children aged between nine and seventeen. Her husband died of malaria and tuberculosis. He was buried at a free cemetery without a tombstone. Her children are at a school where they don't have to pay but she'd like to be able to afford to buy them school uniforms. She has a Katemba where she sells fritters and Freezit (cheap frozen drinks). Sometimes the church helps by donating clothes. Another lady holds a child that has been abused by its father. The child is probably around six but wears a nappy and chews her fingers like a baby. Her hands droop listlessly at the wrists and her head nods downwards as her empty eyes look randomly into space. Yet another tells me she is homeless, her husband having died in 1990. In fact all of her children are also dead and now she's completely alone. As she has no money for rent she has no shelter. She has made a hut from mud with a grass roof but when the rains come the roof leaks and she becomes very muddy. An older man who previously worked as a tractor driver for the government has squandered all his money – he does a bit of farming to try to make ends meet, but even his own children refuse to help him.

Another woman's husband died in 1969, all her children died of AIDS, and she is without work or money. One widow says her daughter who is 22 was formerly renting a room from her but now she has goitre and is very sick – she has been taken to hospital but there's nothing they can do; she has to support her, but there's no food, no hope. A distinguished looking elderly gentleman, dressed in a rather shabby light grey pinstriped suit used to be a businessman until the owner of the business died and everyone wanted to inherit it. The ensuing quarrels and squabbles resulted in nothing being left for anyone. Now he is a beggar.

I am to hear many more stories: Emmanuel is thirteen and in grade four at school. He is on treatment for HIV and is kept by his niece who is single and sells vegetables to earn a living. Lorene is 32 years old. Her children are five, ten and twelve but she also looks after three orphans aged six, eight and ten. She needs help to take the children to school. Christine is a 49-year-old widow whose husband died of ulcers. She has two children who don't go to school because there is no money to pay for their fees. One of the children has a heart condition and needs medical attention. Henry is a 40-year-old bricklayer who is simply looking for a job to support his family. 38-year-old Joyce's husband died six years ago and she has six children to support. And so it goes on.

My next journey is to a tribal village just outside Lusaka, called Chongwe. On the way, I speak to our driver, **Titus**. At 30 years old he has four brothers and two sisters and lives in Condor Square, Lusaka with his wife and children aged 9 and 4. He sounds traumatised at having to recall his childhood. He wasn't brought up with his mother but by her cousin who sponsored him through school. He seems not to want to explain why. His brothers and sisters were brought up with his aunties. His father died a long time ago, he doesn't remember when. One of his brothers died when he was in his 40s – he doesn't know what he died of because he was living elsewhere. Titus has been to many funerals. His best friend died of AIDS and is buried at Leopards Hill. Although Titus helped out and contributed transport and money, there wasn't enough money to buy a tombstone and now the grass is so high nobody can see where the grave is. Titus says he would now go and put a tombstone there if only he knew where the grave was. He's still in touch with his late friend's widow and child. He's very sad for them. To Titus, the most important thing in life is having a good job and he is currently looking for something to help him get a better living. Titus previously worked in South Africa where he was sponsored to learn how to drive a truck. He's currently waiting for another friend of his based in South Africa to find him a new job there. He knows his children would be okay if he had a better job. Like most Zambians Titus attends church every week. His is the Church of God although he says he's a bit sceptical about spirits going up to heaven. Without knowing that the cemetery is already likely to be full and closed Titus believes he'll also be buried at Leopards Hill. He's also convinced he'll be remembered forever *"because I've left my children – people will say, 'That's Titus'."*

We reach Chongwe, after travelling around 30 kilometers down a long straight road and seeing virtually no other cars. A dusty track lined with shack-like shops and open bars forms the main street. We were hoping to be welcomed by the 'chieftainess' of the area – a tribal Queen. As is the custom, we have purchased groceries to present to her majesty consisting of two large bags of sugar, two medium sized plastic bottles of cooking oil and two big bags of maize flour. However it seems that the lady we had planned to meet is busy and we're asked to wait to see her chief adviser. The royal 'palace' is hidden away from the main street and reached by a small alleyway. Just along here is a small bar/restaurant and the village courtroom. The courtroom consists of a small concrete administration office outside which are six courtroom chairs. The metal-framed chairs have green peeling paint and no cushions. When I complain that they're very uncomfortable I'm told that it's to keep the locals awake during court proceedings!

I fear we could be waiting all day for the chief adviser so arrange to speak to someone else who works here. **Christopher** is 59 years old and works as the Senior Chief's Retainer responsible for the security of the chief. Christopher has eleven children and eleven grandchildren. He was one of seven children himself – although now he's the only one left. His siblings have died from a range of disorders which he describes as follows: "*one had things pricking in his stomach, another had heart failure, one had an accident, others had common diseases such as AIDS.*" His own children range from 39 to 11 years of age and they are all still living. His firstborn is a Catholic nun who is now based in Malawi. Unfortunately his wife passed away last month at the age of 56. He's not sure what she died of - there were complications and it was painful for her to eat. She was buried in a communal grave in the village which he still goes to visit but there is no tombstone. People gave donations and, with the help of the chief, the district council and well-wishers, they raised 1,200,000 kwachas (around £200) for a coffin.

His wife's death is the most significant thing that has ever happened to Christopher. She was his best friend and now he's alone wondering how he'll manage without her. "*It's like she's just gone for a visit somewhere and is coming back*," he says. He's talked about it to his friends and his grandchildren. He's a Catholic who goes to church every Sunday although he doesn't believe in an afterlife. Christopher feels that memories linger and even after he dies he'd like to be remembered through photographs of him. Words of wisdom that he'd like to pass on to future generations are: "*work hard, have some place where you can cultivate crops for yourself, rather than depending on others. Work hard at an individual level and keep a surplus, some savings, in reserve for emergencies.*" He'd also like to warn people of the perils of using witchdoctors. "*Some are quacks who offer 'cures' for money. If a woman is barren, a witchdoctor might have sex with her as a cure. Sometimes the husband finds out and this causes lots of trouble. And sometimes the witchdoctor gives poison to his customers.*"

We'd arrived in Chongwe at around 11.00 am and by now it's about 12.30. The adviser we're waiting to see delays us further saying that he'll meet us at a nearby hotel bar shortly. Unfortunately during the lengthy wait that follows I'm compelled to use the hotel's public toilet, which has an open-running sewer outside the door. I squat anxiously anticipating that a black mamba snake will slide through a gap in the corrugated iron roof as school children hiding behind a hedge outside repeatedly chant "*how d'you do.*" We end up waiting until almost 2.00 pm - popularly called Zambian time

Finally, the adviser who is 61 years old and called **John** arrives. John had three brothers of whom two have died from heart attacks – one aged 54 and the other aged 64. He's married with six children aged between 36 and 15. He's been to lots of funerals both in town and village. One of his brothers is buried in a village cemetery and another is buried nearby. Some of his friends have died of AIDS and he's been to many funerals at Leopards Hill in Lusaka. He says, "*It's devastating that you bury someone and after ten years you can't find the grave.*" He thinks the identification of graves should be improved. "*The village cemeteries are much better, there aren't so many in the graveyard. In the villages, the funerals are communal and the approach is very good: They don't care what disease has killed you, whether it be cholera, or AIDS, they tend to the dead regardless. In the town if you die of cholera, they won't go near you.*"

John would like to be buried in the village cemetery where his family can visit. His parents' death was very significant to him. He was particularly sad when his father died from old age. His happiest time was the completion of his schooling and the experience he has had in his working career. He was honoured to be chosen as adviser to a chiefdom of 900,000 people. He'd previously worked in human resources management at the African headquarters of Intercontinental Hotels in Nairobi. Following his retirement he has learned so much about the area's culture and traditional customs during his seven years in his role as adviser. One of the most important customs in this part of Africa is that when people die their heads should face east and their feet should face west in their graves. It's very important that children know this custom, "*otherwise something bad could happen.*" John refers to the local customs as "*intellectual property. We must own this knowledge – it is riches to pass over cultural traditions.*" John would like to be remembered as someone who contributed a lot to his tribe by imparting culture and knowledge, by "*promoting the customary norms of the tribe and their traditional ceremonies.*" He'd like to "*go down in books as a chief adviser who contributed to doing away with the negative cultures that cause AIDS, because I'm educated.*" He'd also like to be remembered by his children, his grandchildren and his great grandchildren. John is a Catholic who attends church every Sunday in addition to other traditional occasions. He is proud that he was baptised at only two weeks old. He's also fortunate that he learned about sexually transmitted diseases and death at school. He strongly believes that heaven and hell are the two places that you can go to after you die. He even believes that "*if someone dies they'll come back as a ghost.*"

John thinks it's very important to have a nice coffin, "*it's a pride to the children.*" He already paid for a deposit on a coffin but unfortunately he was cheated out of the money. He would expect a very good memorial service attended by his whole family and lasting five successive days. If he died today he'd anticipate at least 500,000 mourners would attend his funeral. He's the HIV/AIDS co-ordinator for seven chieftains in the provinces and they would all come with a dedication. His coffin would probably cost around a million kwachas (about £200) and the transport would cost 8-10 million kwachas (approximately £1500-£1800). John's enthusiastic parting words to me were, "*I wish I could die today. I'm at the top of my career. It would be the greatest thing to happen!*"

We travelled past villages of mud huts thatched with straw to deliver some of the gifts of groceries to John's welcoming and polite wife and son. I wasn't sure they'd be quite so enthusiastic about their husband/father's demise.

Back in the centre of Lusaka I met **Eddie**, a well-known Zambian sculptor and musician at his studio. He was born in 1953 and is one of eight children. In 1979 his father who was in his 60's died of asthma. One of his brothers died at the age of six. He was sleeping in bed and was struck by lightening coming in through the window. He died the same day from his burns. It was difficult to accept his death because he was so young. Many people believed that he had died due to black magic. Another brother died at the age of 32 from AIDS. His father and two brothers are all buried at Leopards Hill cemetery. There are no tombstones even though Eddie's a sculptor and is employed to design and create headstones for other people. The graves do have numbers though and are placed alongside that of his grandmother. Eddie normally visits once a year. He mentions the fact that there are more people attending funerals these days mainly because they get fed! Sometimes people come to stay for five days whilst they are waiting for other guests to arrive from the villages. Things are slowly changing because it just costs too much. Eddie's all too aware of the lack of care taken of cemeteries, *"I've seen them in South Africa,"* he says, *"They're so clean you could eat from the graveyard. Here people throw plastics and litter; the council should clean them up, or even the visitors, or both. Lots of people would love to have tombstones, but this is seen as a want, not a need – they are simply too expensive for most people. In Zambia it's also desirable to bury someone in the most beautiful possible coffin – but what about the family left behind? If the parent leaves children of school age, why do they spend so much on a funeral? There are now so many widows and widowers. Families grab everything from the widows and they become poor. The poor children need to go to school – they need better education, better food and better health. The people left to look after them don't even feed them. These just use the children as a bridge to get their parents' wealth. If someone marries a widow, they just do it to get the money – they often end up going back to their former wife and family."*

Eddie is a Christian who goes to church every week and believes in the afterlife. His dream is to set up an art academy catering for young people. "*If you can't take care of young people, our future is doomed,*" he says. They only have one college in Zambia and not everyone can get a place. Young people are mainly to be found in the streets with their small businesses trying to make some money – but many of them want to be artists. No one can help them accomplish their dream. Eddie wants to "*empower young people with skills and knowledge*" and to this end he's already registered his academy as a company and applied for a site to set up the business. He's currently sourcing funding to erect the structures for the academy. He's also training four people to help with his sculpting enterprise.

Eddie's words of wisdom to future generations are to "*look after yourself and stick to what you do in life.*" Eddie's seen many people drop out of the art world – whereas he has stuck it out. Some have passed away, some have changed direction. He says it's been mainly due to money, since when artists have difficult times and don't make much money, they simply give up. He explains, "*They don't understand why they became artists, they don't consider the beauty of art – just the money. Sometimes you can sell and other times you can't. To be an artist you need to love your job and to give it time and commitment. You also have to look at your competitors, what they are producing and where they are failing so you can improve. Look at the finishing and the standards and decide where you are going wrong. Attend workshops, go to school, exchange ideas with other artists and learn from other people.*"

Eddie is married with three sons and two daughters who are all in good health. He's happy he's alive because most of his friends are dead. He says the reason that he's still alive is that he lives on art. He's still producing because he hasn't realized his biggest achievement yet. At one point he thought he had created his greatest sculpture – a carved stone chair for the Catholic cathedral in

Lusaka. He's even won awards and is very pleased to be so appreciated for what he does. But he hopes to do even better in the future.

Eddie has a lot to say about AIDS. Talking about sex used not to be allowed. It's still a taboo subject but nowadays the issue has grown so big that it simply can't be ignored. Almost every family is affected. AIDS has brought misery and created street kids – who have no parents, no education and who have nothing to do except go to the streets and beg. Eddie also tells of his sadness at visiting the University Teaching Hospital where it's horrifying to see how many people are suffering from AIDS. Some die in a very short time but others take six or seven years to go. Sometimes people sell everything before they die to pay for drugs. "*The disease is very expensive,*" he says, "*People need money all the time. Sometimes sufferers become cantankerous and overly demanding. If the breadwinner is sick, the partner is often forced to sell all their worldly goods – their radio, deep freeze, TV set, chairs whatever – or even to go to a witchdoctor to buy a potion that they are told is a cure. Then the person with AIDS dies and their partner is left with nothing.*"

There's also confusion about sex education. People need more education. Some people say that condoms are not good others that they are preventative. Eddie's view is that "*condoms cannot be avoided. They aren't 100% safe because they can break. They're not a cure. They're an alternative, but not a solution.*" Eddie's not taking any drug therapy because he hasn't felt the need yet – although he's started to feel weaker over the past couple of years. If he dies he'd be buried in Leopard's Hill if he were not abroad at the time. He understands though that the cemetery is likely to be closed in a few years time. He thinks they're burying around 75 people a day now and has heard that there's going to be a new cemetery on Michael Galaun's land. The problem's made worse by people moving from other provinces to Lusaka. The townships are growing bigger and bigger.

Eddie returns to the subject closest to his heart and says that Zambians need to market their art to the outside world more effectively. *"There's no national art gallery in Zambia. The Livingstone Museum is better than the Lusaka Museum, yet most people coming to Zambia visit Lusaka. We need a National art gallery for contemporary and fine art and a national theatre complex. The Lusaka Playhouse is nothing. We need more infrastructure for concerts, events; we need to boost the arts here."* Eddie's dream for the national art gallery is to have different sections – one for the art of traditional chiefs with sculptures, stories and information, one for the political heroes of Zambia, one for heads of state including traditional African heroes such as Nelson Mandela and another space for artists in residence to work on the site as well as a gallery for sales and a library for local and visiting students. I am inspired not only by Eddie's obvious creative talent but also by his sense of vision and purpose. I like his work and may even buy one of his sculptures for my London terrace though they're not cheap even by Western standards. I'm beginning to realise how essential money is. So is it money that buys immortality, I find myself asking … money for a plot of land in a cemetery; money for a tombstone and money for a national museum of art?

One person who I will always remember from my trip to Zambia is **Victor**. A modest 36 year old man with a lovely African smile and an unusually philosophical approach to life. Victor is a highly educated man – a conservation forester, specialising in agriculture, forestry and rural development. He's also an expert on Zambian plants and trees – including the medicinal uses of plants and vegetation, of which I get a running commentary on every flower, bush and tree in our vicinity. He lives with his wife and three children aged eleven, seven and three. His wife runs a stationery and Internet business. They employ a relative as a maid – she was in a difficult situation – it would have been very easy for her to have become pregnant as early as twelve years old. She works for them during the day and goes to college in the evenings.

Victor comes from a large family, citing three sisters and six brothers, three aunts, four uncles, ten cousins and three second cousins. His father, two sisters and two brothers have died. His father, who was sixty six years old died from a horrific form of bone cancer where his bones visibly rotted away. His brother Joseph died at the age of thirty six after being involved in a hit and run incident with a vehicle and another brother Adams at the age of twenty nine – Victor says his death was due to depression. He wanted to pursue his own career but there were no resources to enable him to do so. His elder sister Jane and younger sister, Nello (who died at the age of fourteen), have also passed away due to *"unexplained complications within their body chemistry."* I ask Victor for more information about the causes of his sisters' deaths but he insists that they died due to complications and will say no more than that. I am left to draw my own conclusions.

Victor explains how powerless he felt at the time of each death. He had such a great feeling of loss but there was nothing he could do to help. He turned to his wife and children for comfort. He says, *"I remember them by what they did and aspired to do, as well as remembering the good things and times spent together."* He has named his third son after Adams, *"as a source of inspiration and means of bringing him back."* He sees funerals as a way of paying last respects and consoling surviving relatives. But as well as sympathy there's also material and financial support to the bereaved family. *"Cemeteries are sacred places where loved ones are resting. Unfortunately, in my country, a great many of them are not well kept ... it makes me sad to see such neglect."* Victor is also saddened by the practice of grabbing property at the expense of surviving spouses and children, *"death is a mystery and only God knows what happens,"* he says, *"I would like to see relatives respecting the wishes of those who have passed on."* Victor believes that *"everyone is your brother, sister, mother, father, uncle and aunt to whom you can turn in time of need..."* He's not deeply religious, but adds, *"I am a firm believer in God Almighty, through Jesus Christ our Lord and Saviour... I believe in the teachings of the Bible about life after salvation, attained through the serving knowledge of the Lord Jesus."*

To Victor, his family is everything. He explains that both his mother and his wife have always been resourceful, *"with a deep-seated platform of love and care."* His wife and children are his closest friends and companions. He would hate them ever to be mistreated and wants them to *"perpetuate the legacy of my hard work for my community, country and world."* Victor is well aware of his humble beginnings and recognises that all he has is the result of hard work and dedication to duty. Victor is keen to improve his education further as well as that of his wife and children. His mother came from a royal family in Zambia but she left home to avoid an arranged marriage. His parents' philosophy and way of life had a strong part to play in forming his life. During his childhood, *"children had to be like servants to their parents and do everything for themselves. Nowadays, children are able to watch television, to use computers and they all seem to want to have very expensive things."*

Victor was a clever child who was lucky enough to be sent to a leading college in Livingstone. He was expected to become a mechanical engineer but disagreed with his lecturers about his future career and left college before graduating. He joined the military and became a first lieutenant flying MiGS. He was sent to Russia in 1990 and then to West Germany where he was able to study for a degree in geography and land use at the same time as continuing with his flight training. Victor received a bolt from the blue when his flight commander suddenly announced that he didn't think Victor was suitable for the military. Apparently he wasn't really the right sort of person to be a soldier and it was probably better that he concentrate on finishing his studies. Fortunately Victor was given the opportunity to finish his studies in Zambia, enabling him to become a leading forestry and land-use expert there.

Victor's favourite proverb is: *Make the wise your companion and you grow wise yourself. Make fools your friends and suffer for it.* When he dies, Victor would like as much as can reasonably be afforded to be spent on his funeral and memorial service *"with Christian music, gospel and biblical teachings."* But Victor is also likely to be remembered through his own botanical and geographical reference works..... and incredibly, as I discover, through a book currently being written by someone who was once very close to him: a tale of racial tension and unfulfilled love that sounds like it has the potential not only to be a best seller but also a major feature film.

Transcendence
Expressions of Eternal Love

Contemplating death pushes us beyond all definitions of human knowledge and into realms that are as yet impossible to quantify. Yet thoughts, feelings and emotions that come from our indirect experience of death are all encompassing – pain, anger, despair, wonderment, serenity, sadness, relief, hope, love and confusion - to name just a few. Some of us believe that the spirit lives on after death, that we are reincarnated, or will go heaven, or hell. Others of us believe that there is simply nothing beyond this life. Whichever of these beliefs we hold our immortality is often assured through expressions ranging from grief and hopelessness to eternal love for us when we have departed. We are also immortalised through our own thoughts, feelings, hopes and fears, as expressed through artistic, literary, scientific, community-based, or humanitarian endeavours. Some of us live on via our tributes to us, whether they be creations of music, art, poetry, sculpture, architecture, charity fund-raising events, two-minutes silence, or simply words on a memorial website.

The main way in which we transcend death is through others' memories of us. It is now thought that not only the brain but also the heart stores memories. Over the last 40 years, since heart transplants have been conducted, a significant number of people receiving new hearts have noticed changes in their personality and memories linked to those of the heart donor. Research by Professor Pearsall and Gary Schwartz at Yale University has led to new ideas that the heart has its own form of intelligence and that heart neurones have short and long term memory, just like those in the brain. The heart is in constant communication with the brain, but the magnetic energy of the heart is five thousand times more powerful than that of the brain. According to the

Institute of Heart Math in California, the heart can think for itself and is a place of memories. It is hardly surprising then that we have such heartfelt feelings when someone who is dear to us dies.

When a close friend or relative departs from this world, there is often a requirement to express the physicality of our pain. The fact that such strong physical manifestations of pain are felt often comes as a surprise to the bereaved. To many the heaviness caused by the gap in their life could easily be described as having a broken heart. Jeffrey Caine, the writer of the screenplay for *The Constant Gardener* still feels the pain of his wife's death ten years on. He tells *the Sunday Times, "I haven't got over her death. I still grieve her loss, her absence... The pain doesn't go away. Nothing helps; nothing compensates for her not being here."* He says he identifies with words from a film called *Shadowlands*, which tells the story of C S Lewis and his love for a woman who becomes terminally ill. When she's dying she says to him *"We can't have the happiness of yesterday without the pain of today – that's the deal."* The strength of our feelings about death has resulted in some of our best-loved works of music, poetry and literature. One could fill a book with sublime examples – from Mozart's *Requiem* to Shakespeare's *Romeo and Juliet*. However in the Western world, the currency of today's expression is more likely to mix celebrity autobiographies and new age interpretations of the mystery of death with populist outpourings of feeling.

Douglas J Davies points out *"If technology continues to advance, society enhancing expertise is likely to be grasped and developed by the young in a society that inverts the age-respect values of traditional societies in which wisdom accrued through long years of experience. Accordingly, the death of the young, or the very young, by contrast, will be deemed a shame. Young children and, even more so young adults who possess extensive networks of significance will be mourned intensively."* This was certainly the case when 17-year old Anna Svidersky was stabbed to death in a small-town American restaurant. When friends decided to compose an online tribute with a collage of photographs, thousands of people were suddenly mourning a girl they had never met. There was talk of making virtual pilgrimages to Anna's web page. Some even wrote songs or made video tributes in dedication. Thousands of messages in tribute to the late Anna started with *"I didn't know you, but..."*

In 2004 the think tank, Civitas, produced a report on the way British people reacted to events such as Princess Diana's death and the Soham murders. They termed the mass outpouring of grief 'mourning sickness'. Their report claims that in making false connections with strangers, people are actually grieving for sadness inside themselves and attaching these feelings to a well-known face or event. Tim Jonze, writing about the case in *the Guardian* says, *"Certainly, in an age where chat rooms and 'virtual' friends are replacing traditional support structures such as religion and the family, the need to make emotional connections is stronger than ever, even if they are not genuine."* He goes on to describe an almost competitive element as to who can grieve the most hysterically... *"Maybe they think it will get them more online friends,"* he adds, *"The grim truth is that this tragedy has mutated into the latest Internet buzz."* This has even extended to players of role-playing games on the Internet using Anna's picture in their online games. Is this a useful expression of immortality, or does it set a dangerous precedent?

Cancer blogging has become a widespread phenomenon. In a trend set by John Diamond recounting his battle with throat cancer weekly in *the Times*, the

Vogue journalist, Deborah Hutton, who died of lung cancer at the age of 49, Julia Darling, a writer and poet who died to breast cancer at 48 and others, such as leukaemia sufferer, Michael Durham, have all written of their experiences in weblogs. Neil Hughes' weblog, www.samanthahughes.info, chronicling his three year old daughter's treatment for a particularly aggressive form of cancer, *neuroblastoma*, is particularly heart wrenching. Hughes says the blog is therapeutic, *"it's a way of dealing with it and channelling my energy. When she first became ill we sought information from the Internet.We were able to contact other parents of sick children and their stories helped us."* There are also practical reasons for this particular weblog – to raise awareness of this rare condition so that other children are diagnosed earlier – and to encourage blood donors. Deborah Hutton's book, *What Can I Do To Help?* , published a day before her death also offers *"75 practical ideas for family and friends from cancer's frontline."* The book gives advice about the ways in which cancer patients can be helped by those around them and all the author's royalties go to the hospice charity, Macmillan Cancer Relief.

Others are immortalised through charities and events that raise money for fatal conditions and diseases. Many have donated legacies for setting up charitable foundations devoted to medical research, or simply helping others. These often flourish with the help of celebrity endorsement or patronage of fund raising events. Celebrity victims of preventable or potentially curable diseases such as heart disease and cancer have established charities for their cause – such as www.caronkeating.org. But it's not just celebrities who want to be remembered for their time spent on this planet. The website of the Roy Castle Lung Cancer Foundation says: '*Tribute Funds are a positive and simple way for friends and family to remember a loved one and, in their name, help fund vital research* into early detection and treatment of lung cancer. In recent years, an increasing number of people have decided to remember someone special by making gifts in their name to The Roy Castle Lung Cancer Foundation. These are special and meaningful gifts.

Many of our supporters have told us they would like to continue to support the Foundation in the name of their loved one, as a very positive way to keep their spirit alive, and at the same time support our vital research to help future generations. With this in mind, we have established a very special opportunity called Tribute Funds. Kay Williams lost her father to lung cancer in 2003. "Opening a Tribute Fund in memory of my Dad, Alan Arthur, was a wonderful way to keep his memory alive. He will always be in my heart but this Tribute Fund will help achieve positive results from something negative. It is a way to say, "This is for you, Dad" but also to help others along the way. Thank you so much for giving me somewhere to put my energy and grief. It's an unexpected opportunity. This has given me a great sense of achievement. I desperately wanted to do something positive for Dad. I feel I have and now look forward to watching the Fund grow from strength to strength. Dad would be delighted".'

For some, writing about their feelings of bereavement can serve both as a dedication to their partner and a way of sharing immortality with them. Joan Didion, in her book, *The Year of Magical Thinking*, wanted to represent the struggle of the intellect to contain the madness of grief over her husband, John's, death. She describes the book as "*My attempt to make sense of the period that followed, weeks and months that cut loose any fixed idea I had ever had about death, about illness, about probability and luck, about good fortune and bad, about marriage and children and memory, about grief, about the ways in which people do and do not deal with the fact that life ends, about he shallowness of sanity, about life itself.*"

One of the ways in which we give meaning to life is by bringing sanctity to death through a funeral, or dedicated memorial service. Remembrance park designer, Donald Boddy's job is to make the memorial environment sacred. He says, *"Before I design a new park, I have to understand the site – to understand its environment and landscape – to me this is the most important keys to unlocking the senses to create a feeling of sense of place… Each tree, plant, garden or sculpture we create should have a story of symbolism in mythology, medicine, history, religion, music, art and culture."* He explains that art, music, colour and smell are particularly important elements. *"At the West Pennine Park, we have a herbal garden to aid remembering – these are scents associated with people and location. How many of you remember your grand parents using Lavender soap or oils? "* Music is also a great aid to memory – we all have sounds associated with people and different events throughout our lives. Donald holds musical events throughout the summer in his remembrance parks, where people came come and have a picnic in the park. *"What would you say if I invited you to come and listen to a concert and have a picnic with me in a cemetery?"* asks Donald *"You would question my sanity!"* This is because there is a problem with the word cemetery and its connotations – the word park is somehow acceptable. If you ask a religious person what would make a place sacred to them they would normally mention a religious symbol such as a cross, a Jewish person might think of a Star of David. Symbols and art are also highly significant for the emotions and memories they create. Colour is another major memory trigger, affecting our moods and our whole perception of a place – making us recall happy and sad times alike. There is a difference between fields of wild poppies, orchards of flowering cherries and regimentally ordered flowerbeds, for instance. Donald says that as there is really no official blueprint, he has had to create his own formula for what represents sacred in terms of a memorial garden.

The treatment of immortality through expressions such as art, music, architecture and gardens has changed throughout the ages. The portrayal of the dead has often been in a religious context. From Handel to Britten, requiem masses have harmoniously expressed a faith that those who have died will rest in peace. Love of those departed is also immortalised through musical dedications to those who were loved – from *Greensleeves* to the Beatles' *Michelle* and beyond these lovers will be remembered forever. Contrast this with modern day rap and hip-hop music that glamorises gun culture, drugs and gratuitous sex - and where those most revered are murdered gang leaders, or top selling hip-hop artists, such as Tupac Shakur.

By the time he was 20, Tupac had been arrested eight times, even serving eight months in prison after being convicted of sexual abuse. In addition, he was the subject of two wrongful-death lawsuits, one involving a six-year-old boy who was killed after getting caught in gang-war crossfire between Shakur's gang and a rival group. He later survived being shot five times in an armed robbery before being killed by unknown gunmen in September 1996, at the age of only 25. There are many websites dedicated to his memory and Tupac has become something of a martyr to the cause of helping kids who hang out on the streets and get into trouble. In 1997, his mother set up The Tupac Amaru Shakur Foundation and launched an arts centre to help young people express themselves through music, dance and drama. Whilst Tupac's creative legacy lives on to benefit future generations, he is remembered by his friend, Shock G, who fondly recalls *"Pac would spend entire days in the studio, drinking Hennessy, smoking marijuana, and experimenting with new raps."*

The thing about music, art, sporting achievements, literature, humanitarian acts, poetry and even smells is that they transcend death, but do they transcend the individual and their story? Our personal upbringing, culture and life experiences certainly no longer matter when we are remembered only by the concerto we composed, the song we sang together, or the music played at our funeral. But is death the great leveller, or is there a pecking order as to how we are remembered? How do we compare the dead? Some, such as Shakespeare and Mozart are attributed with enormous achievements in their respective fields; others are bestowed posthumous honours, even sainthoods, for their contribution to humanity; some leave physical reminders of their presence, such as Prince Albert's Royal Albert Hall, or Albert Memorial in London; significant and powerful people's lives are often recorded in history books or biographies; whilst some may even become the stuff of legend – take the conspiracy theories about Marilyn Monroe's death and Princess Diana's untimely end… Many of us may leave just a few photos.

What will your gift to future generations be?

We are only just beginning to realise the sense of isolation and loss caused by our relatively newfound individual independence. With the demise of the nuclear family unit and the erosion of family values, other communities are now emerging in response to the fragmentation in our lives caused by lack of emotional interaction.

Far removed from their virtual, 3-D counterparts, new communities such as book clubs, debating forums, networking groups and charities are flourishing as we all reach out to be loved and appreciated for our opinions, personalities, artistic, sporting, business and humanitarian endeavours. Many of us have started to wonder about the purpose of our lives. Is it simply to procreate? Is it to make as much money as possible? What will be the sum total of your life on this planet? The explosion in autobiographies, biographical accounts, reality TV, Tracey Emin's bed and celebrity obsession are all by-products of our desire to each be remembered for our unique contribution to society. Now there is also a way of being remembered forever through the Internet. Free online memorial sites and digital time capsules will enable every one of us to be represented how we or others would like to remember – to transcend the present and leave our personal legacy for future generations, to make of it what they will.

My study of trends in death turned out to be a contemplation of immortality: A life-consuming search affecting every human being. There are many ways of being remembered for a long time - through your successors, your achievements and good works, through gravestones and monuments to your memory – but, it seems clear to me, that the best hope we now have of being remembered forever is through the Internet. In a way, the memory of the dead never dies so long as it is kept alive by the living. And the dead can be an inspiration to future generations so long as they *are* remembered.

A Look Beyond Physical Matter

The Key to Everlasting Life?

Everything changes, but God changes not. (Words from the hymn, Gun Hill) The Roman Catholic Church hasn't changed much over the years and when Pope Benedict XVI took office, he announced he stood for 'no change' in a world of extreme change. No change on the Church's views on contraception and abortion in particular. So what about this? How does this sit alongside all that we are going through in terms of social transition and dramatic techno-logical transformation? What is really important in life?

Natural disasters of the enormity of the December 2004 tsunami and hurri-cane Katrina in September 2005, as well as terrorist atrocities such as suicide bombings in on 9/11 in New York and 7/7 in London make us realise that, wherever we are in the world, the most significant thing is our love for our fellow men, women and children.

If we consider what is important on an individual level the things that come immediately to mind are: – someone to love, somewhere to live, something to do and something to look forward to. Sex, money and mortality are key aspects of all of our lives. If we consider what's important on a more general level, it's having essentials such as food, water, fuel and a means of communi-cation (which in this day and age means Internet access!)

I believe we will eventually realise that we have enough money to enable every single person the world over to have free access to basic needs such as water, grain/rice, a cheap local energy supply and a means of transmitting messages and information to each other. Frenchman, Louis-Sebastian Mercier, published a work in 1770 called '*L'an 2440, reve s'il en fut jamais*' which became probably the first best-selling work about the future. His prognosis for a perfect world of peaceful nations, constitutional leaders, universal education and racial equality is still possible by the year 2440.

Not much has really changed over the centuries of our existence. We have and always will be human beings with our own peculiar ways, wants and needs. In our new peaceful world, every one of us will still be different. Our unique inequality will be what we are remembered by. I am sure that in the future, we will start to look more to the past for inspiration. History and historians will regain prominence. Antiques, old books, parts of the world that have been long forgotten such as China, Egypt and South America will gain popularity. Biographies, autobiographies, online diaries, obituaries and blogs will capture our attention.

The Internet will be the crucial key in enabling these changes to take place. In the words of Jean Houston in her book, *Jump Time*, "*the Internet is returning to individuals much of the authority lost to institutions during the explosion of industrialization. Suddenly you have more control over information and resources, a development that is already playing havoc with traditional top-down government, business, even religion.*" Houston sees this as "*a revolution in autonomy as well as responsibility... Densely interconnected communication networks of people who cherish their communities and care deeply about life on this planet are creating something never seen before: a meta-sphere of governance...This movement involves every area of the Earth in a conscious, self-organizing, life-serving, planetary process. The Earth herself is becoming a vast teaching-learning community, a new order of democratic biology, as individuals and groups learn as they participate and create together a new arena for social evolution."*

The mind and the soul are things of the future. Bodies don't really matter and this will become all too evident once not only cosmetic alteration and enhancement but human cloning also becomes commonplace. The mind is unique and original and the soul is the essence of being. The body is simply the receptacle in which these are housed. Research for the first part of this book led me to investigate attempts to map the human mind, its feelings and emotions. Surely then it is only a short step to exploring the possibility of survival of the human personality after death? I am reminded of the wonderful 1946 film, *A Matter of Life and Death,* starring David Niven as a young fighter pilot who arrives back after a raid in the fog and is caught between two worlds, one of which only exists in the mind. Is the authenticity of our mortality merely something of our own imagining?

In the near-term, some of the world's population may continue to focus on material aggrandisement and bodily perfection, but those with more foresight and education will look beyond for something more meaningful. A breed of physically stronger people could emerge with uses for manual labour, where necessary - and as providers of sperm for future mixed race generations. Eventually, race will become irrelevant, as everyone will be appreciated for who they are – not just in terms of their appearance, but much more for the power of their mind and for the level of their soul's development.

Individuals of the human race will regain their place in society and celebrate their part and their achievements. In the future, there will be room for everyone. After the much more competitive times we have experienced in past decades, a new status quo will emerge. People will learn to respect each other, despite their differences, and to realise that we are all sharing this planet together. The great illusion of human nature is that people are the same. We are all different, but we are all human: Just as man is different from woman, Catholic from Jew or Muslim, poor from middle class from super rich ... We are all different, and rightly so – we should cherish and nurture our differences from white to black, including all the shades in between.

But please note that, just as there is inequality in life, so there is inequality in death - a better handbag may equate to a bigger tombstone when you are gone! In an age where consumer brands wield such tremendous power we are just beginning to experience the emergence of designer funerals. This will be a major new growth area.

Ultimately of course what you buy is what anyone with same amount of money can get ...it's what you do that really makes a difference. I foresee an increasing desire to leave our personal imprint on this world and make a lasting impression after we have died. But do heed the words of the Dalai Lama "*At the beginning of our life is birth, during which we suffer, and at the end of our life is death, during which we also suffer. Between these come ageing and illness. No matter how wealthy you are or how physically fit you are, you have to suffer through these circumstances.*" And then you die.

So whilst you're awaiting immortality, why not appreciate who you are by enjoying yourself to the best of your ability...of course you will be doing good works for a major karmic reward, because whatever we have done in our lives makes us what we are when we die – and absolutely everything counts!

Despite advances in modern medicine, it's really the quality of life rather than the length that matters. As Abraham Lincoln said *"In the end, it's not the years in your life that count. It's the life in your years."*

Thanks to our music, art, fashion, literature, sports, poetry, textures, scents, memories … and, ultimately the Internet, (where, sooner or later, we will be able to record all of these things), we can transcend our differences and continue to enhance the lives of others long after we are gone. We will each be remembered for our contribution to the future of mankind. We are all futurologists – it's our own foresight, wisdom and intuition that guides us what to do.

The future belongs to us all.

Life is no 'brief candle' to me.
It is a sort of splendid torch
which I have got hold of
for the moment
and I want to make it burn
as brightly as possible
before handing it on
to future generations.

George Bernard Shaw

BIBLIOGRAPHY

Atlas, James, *My Life in the Middle Ages: A Survivor's Tale,* Harper Collins, 2005

Broderick, Damien, *The Spike: How our Lives are Being Transformed by Rapidly Advancing Technologies,* Tor Books 2002

Castronova, Edward, *Virtual Worlds: A First-hand Account of Market and Society on the Cyberian Frontier,* Indiana University - Dept of Telecommunications; centre for Economic Studies and fo Institute for Economic Research, 2001

Ferrazzi, Keith, *Never Eat Alone,* Currency Doubleday (Random House), 2005

Friedman, Thomas L, *The World is Flat: A Brief History of the Twenty-first Century,* Farrar Straus Giroux, 2005

Furedi, Frank, *The Politics of Fear: Beyond Left and Right,* Continuum International Publishing Group – Academi, 2005

Gladwell, Malcolm, *The Tipping Point: How Little Things Can Make a Big Difference,* Abacus 2002

Harra, Carmen, *Everyday Karma, How to change your life by changing your karma,*
Piatkus, 2002

Holden, Robert, *Success Intelligence: Timeless Wisdom for a Manic Society,* Hodder Mobius, 2005

In Praise of Slow, How a Worldwide Movement is Challenging the Cult of Speed, Orion, 2004

Houston, Jean, *Jump Time – Shaping Your Future in a World of Radical Change,* Sentient Publications, 2004

Daniel Jones, *Bastard On the Couch,* Harper Paperbacks, 2005

Jones, Professor Steve, *Y: The Descent of Me,* Abacus 2003

Kunstler, James Howard, *The Long Emergency,* Atlantic Books, 2005

Kurzweil, Ray, *The Age of Spiritual Machines: How we will Live, Work and Think in the New Age of Intelligent Machines,* Texere Publications USA, 2001

Lee, Susan et al, *Fashioning the Future,* Thames and Hudson, 2005

Lennon, J Robert, *Mailman,* Granta, 2003

Lovelock, James, *The Revenge of Gaia:Why the Earth is Fighting Back and How We Can Still Save Humanity*, Allen Lane/Penguin 2005

Mamen, Maggie, *The Pampered Child Syndrome: How to Recognise It, How to Manage It and How to Avoid It: A Guide to Parents and Professionals*, Jessica Kingsley Publishers, 2005

Margolis, Jonathan, *A Brief History of Tomorrow - the future, past and present* Bloomsbury Publishing, 2000

Moravec, Hans, *Robot, Mere Machine to Transcendent Mind*, Oxford University Press, USA, 2000

Nathanson, Paul and Young, Katherine, *Spreading Misandry:The Teaching of Contempt for Men in Popular Culture*, McGill-Queens University Press, 2002

Noble, Ron, *HIV & AIDS in Zambia – the Epidemic and its Impact*, www.avert.org

Orwell, George, *1984*, Penguin Modern Classics, 2004

Patel, Ketan, *The Master Strategist: Power, Purpose and Principle in Action*, Random House Business Books, 2005

Popcorn, Faith and Hanft, Adam, *Dictionary of the Future:The Words, Terms and Trends that Define theWay We'll Live,Work and Talk*, Hyperion, 2002

Rinpoche, Sogyal, *The Tibetan Book of Living and Dying*, revised ed., HarperSanFrancisco, 2002

M Scott Peck, *The Different Drum:The Creation of True Community – The First Step to World Peace*, Arrow, 1990

Spender, Lizzie, *Wild Horse Diaries*, John Murray, 2005

Strauss, Neil, *The Game: Undercover in the Secret Society of Pick-Up Artists*, Canongate Books Ltd, 2005

Toffler, Alvin, *Future Shock*, Pan, 1973